James W. Hamilton

NEEDLEWORK
FOR STUDENT TEACHERS

SIR ISAAC PITMAN & SONS, Ltd.
PITMAN HOUSE, PARKER STREET, KINGSWAY, LONDON, W.C.2
THE PITMAN PRESS, BATH
PITMAN HOUSE, LITTLE COLLINS STREET, MELBOURNE

ASSOCIATED COMPANIES

PITMAN PUBLISHING CORPORATION
2 WEST 45TH STREET, NEW YORK
205 WEST MONROE STREET, CHICAGO

SIR ISAAC PITMAN & SONS (CANADA), Ltd.
(INCORPORATING THE COMMERCIAL TEXT BOOK COMPANY)
PITMAN HOUSE, 381–383 CHURCH STREET, TORONTO

MADE IN GREAT BRITAIN AT THE PITMAN PRESS, BATH
C7—(H.814)

NEEDLEWORK FOR STUDENT TEACHERS

INTENDED FOR THE USE OF TEACHERS AND STUDENTS OF ALL GRADES

BY

AMY K. SMITH

ELEVENTH EDITION

LONDON
SIR ISAAC PITMAN & SONS, LTD.
1937

PUBLISHERS' NOTE

THE several editions through which this book has passed have provided occasions for bringing the text up to date in small details. In the main, the book remains unaltered, as a simple, clear exposition of the fundamental principles of elementary needlework. It makes no pretence to teach the "decorative Stitchery" or "do-as-you-please" methods of modern times, which are so often over-rated as educative factors.

A sound general knowledge of plain needlework is a necessity to every student of the subject, and equipped with this as a foundation, all new schemes and systems fall into their rightful place, viz. a subsidiary position.

As a means of teaching good methods, and helping students to grasp the solid, sensible facts of an art which never loses its intrinsic value, this volume will always fulfil its purpose as a Standard Textbook for the Student Teacher.

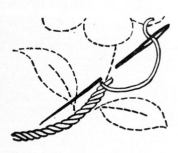
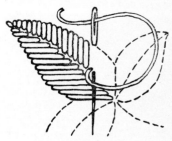

CONTENTS

PART I

STITCHES AND PROCESSES USED IN THE MAKING OF GARMENTS

vii

PART II

PART III

DARNING

PART I

STITCHES AND PROCESSES USED IN THE
MAKING OF GARMENTS

NEEDLEWORK

FOR

STUDENT TEACHERS

APPARATUS FOR TEACHING PURPOSES

IT is now generally agreed that the most successful system of teaching needlework is that known as the " Demonstration Method." By this plan, large numbers can be instructed simultaneously, while it is as easy to teach thirty pupils as one, provided a teacher is master of her subject, and has that essential qualification—confidence. Each member of the class has the privilege of seeing the principles of the work she may have in hand, illustrated on a large scale, by means of some piece of apparatus.

All stitches, especially those worked upon the flat, viz., stitching, herring-boning, button-holing, gathering, running, marking, feather-stitching, knotting ; also darning on material, can be shown, enlarged in size on coarsely and loosely woven fabric.

A chequered blackboard is a useful addition to needlework apparatus. The whole surface of the board should be divided into inch squares. To facilitate counting, it is advisable to have every ¼ yd. coloured differently. Any ordinary board can be made use of by a teacher who does not mind a little trouble. A small tin of enamel will be sufficient to chequer a board 36 by 30 in. The inches should first be faintly marked, and then carefully painted.

Portable black canvas on rollers, divided similarly to the boards, is very convenient for teaching purposes.
These rolls cost from 12s. upwards, according to size.

" Home-made " Apparatus.

1. *Very* coarse towelling or Hessian, coloured thick yarn, upholsterer's cord, or wool, with a large chenille, packing or sail needle, is an excellent means of showing the step-wise succession of each stage of work, and the prepared specimens are always useful for future service.

2. Diagrams drawn with chalk on large sheets of brown paper afford a most inexpensive means of illustrating any

3

process of work. Much time is saved as the sheets can be preserved for future class use if rolled up, and they can be pinned to the blackboard when required.

3. Paper of various kinds can always be selected for illustrating any work on a flat surface. A careful teacher can use paper most successfully, and produce capital results at a very slight expense.

With the above-mentioned apparatus from which to make a selection, no teacher can say that the subject of needlework has not been catered for exhaustively by those who have proved, by experience, that it is only by method and system that a maximum of work can be obtained by a minimum of labour.

CHAPTER I

HINTS TO STUDENTS

General Remarks.—The notes contained in this chapter are intended for those students who are practising with an examination in view ; and although each should work with a higher motive than that of inspection, still one cannot help giving the matter just a thought now and again.

Needlework is an *art*, and, as such, of necessity needs a proportionately greater amount of *time* spent upon it than a subject which requires mental attention alone ; for, if intelligently taught and practised, needlework calls into play both mind and fingers. For the sake of comparison, we may view work under two phases—" specimen " and " practical household." The former should be done to the *very best* of the student's ability, and looked upon as a pattern for others to imitate ; necessarily, it is rather a slow process, as *quality* is the essential. The latter kind of work, although exactly the same in principle, invariably means *quantity* as the first consideration, hence the reason for making this slight distinction.

It is impossible to produce a satisfactory result, unless *steady* and *regular* practice is maintained. *Few* people are perfect needlewomen born, but *many* have taste and skill, which, with cultivation, can be developed to almost any extent, by the exercise of patience, perseverance, and a little exertion—three pre-eminent virtues in any occupation, or in any sphere of life.

Many young teachers fail to produce their best when required, not so much from a lack of knowledge, but from a want of method of showing the ability they possess to the best advantage. It is with the intention of helping to overcome this obstacle that the following chapters are written.

It must be borne in mind that *quantity of work, as well as quality*, is an essential at an examination, and upon the right application of these two features each candidate's merits are assessed.

MATERIALS NECESSARY FOR PRACTICE WORK.

Calico, flannel, print, casement cloth, muslin, stocking-web, and coarse linen are the fabrics usually employed for illustrating the various processes used in needlework. As students are often in doubt as to material suitable for their use, the following may prove helpful—

Calico.—A soft make with even threads should be chosen.

5

6

A1 and B1 are suitable for practice purposes. H, M², and MT for garments.

There are stouter makes of calicoes, suitable for coarser work.

The above longcloths are undoubtedly the best for school and home use, the finish being excellent and the wear everything that could be desired.

Flannel.—Flannel varies in price from 1s. 11d. to 5s. 6d. per yard, or more. There are several kinds—Welsh, Saxony, ·Yorkshire, Lancashire, etc.

Welsh. For wear, perhaps this is unequalled. It is coarse and rough-looking, but very durable. The selvedge or " list " is of a dark grey colour.

Saxony. This is a softer and lighter make, with a pinkish edge. It is used for babies' flannels.

Yorkshire. This is creamy-white in colour, with a very narrow selvedge of black lines. The threads of this make are very clear and distinct. It shows up the work to good effect, and is specially recommended for practice purposes.

Lancashire, as the name implies, is a mixture of cotton and wool. It is similar in colour to Welsh, but with a smoother appearance and more even threads.

Prints.—Choose one with as little dress as possible. For a patch, a pattern needing a little matching should be selected. Zephyrs tobralcos, and ginghams are also recommended for frocks.

Casement Cloths (31, 50, 54 in. wide) are frequently used, and light colours are recommended.

Muslin.—Cambric, nainsook, and mull muslin are suitable for frocks and pinafores. Embroidery cambric is over 40 in. wide.

Stocking-web for darning purposes. Three sizes can be bought —fine, medium, coarse. Web is woven in a circular strip. Medium is recommended for practice.

Linen for marking and darning. Various materials from a common kitchen dowlas to Saxony cloth or Oxford shirting (white) are sold for this purpose. Prominent and even threads are necessary. *Coarse* table linen is very suitable.

Messrs. Cox & Co., 99 and 101 New Oxford Street, W.C.1. also keep a large variety of cloths for darning purposes.

ACCESSORIES.

Cottons.—It is advisable to use coloured cottons for practice work, as the stitches are shown to better effect—hence it is a proper schooling towards excellence. The following grades are generally adopted by those who have had experience in systemizing : Black, blue, or blue-green, pink, and white.

Red cotton is rarely used now, since it is the colour that has been so much condemned by oculists.

Cream cotton is recommended for working on green material, and *green* cotton on cream material.

Embroidery cotton should be used for darning on cotton stocking-web, as it answers the purpose better than Angola mending.

Crochet cotton, Nos. 16, 18 and 20, are recommended for ordinary cloths, 22 and 24 for fine materials.

There are so many good makers of cotton that it is almost impossible to give any preference.

Flourishing or flax thread is used for darning on linen. Coloured thread is recommended for school use.

Needles.—*Betweens* sewing needles are suitable for school use : Nos. 5 and 6 for beginners and 7, 8, and 9 for ordinary use : Nos. 5, 6 and 7 for darning. Wool and crewel needles are often useful in plain work.

Scissors.—Cutting out—medium size—buttonhole.

Pins.—Lillikins are preferred for specimen work, as the mark left is hardly noticeable. Short whites are also necessary.

Knitting Pins.—Nos. 12 to 15 are sizes in ordinary use.
Messrs. Stratton & Co. supply " Stratnoid " sets of rustless pins and thimbles.

Buttons.—Unpierced, and the best quality linen, are cheapest in the end.

Tapes of various widths.—*Linen* tape should be used for all good specimen work.

Inchtape.

Thimble.—For strength and durability the " Dorcas " thimble is unequalled. It is made in three parts, the inner and outer being silver and the intermediate steel. It is thoroughly recommended. Its cost is trifling compared with its comfort and strength.

Wool.—So many kinds are in common use with which all workers are familiar.

PREPARATION OF MATERIAL FOR CUTTING-OUT.

One of the first points to be mastered in teaching cutting-out is what is known as the " way of the stuff." Too much importance cannot be placed upon this, as in criticising garments it ranks before the stitches used in the making up. All woven material consists of two sets of threads, viz., warp or " *selvedge* " and " *weft* " or woof threads (the italicised words are the ones in general use, and should be familiar terms with every seamstress).

Selvedge threads are the longitudinal threads which run from end to end of a fabric, and are tightly wound on rollers in the loom and kept at regularly spaced distances by the healds and reed, so that the warp threads are subjected to the utmost tension. The *weft* thread is wound on a bobbin, which is enclosed in a shuttle and, by the mechanical action of the arms of the loom, passes backwards and forwards alternately over and under the warp threads, according to the pattern to be woven. It is the turning of the " weft " thread in the process of weaving which forms the selvedge. If the weft threads were sufficiently strong (such is rarely the case), they might be unravelled for hundreds of yards. The excellence of the make of material is often shown by the even quality of the selvedge. Silks frequently have coloured selvedges. In flannels it is pink, grey, or dark blue, and varies in width.

Selvedge is sometimes written " selvage." The former is the more correct spelling. The word really means self-edge (*i.e.*, its own edge), which forms a border to the material and extends throughout its length.

The following are a few ways of distinguishing the selvedge—

1. Take the edge of the material between the thumb and finger of the right hand, and at a distance of a few inches away, hold the material with the left thumb and finger. Gently pull the hands in opposite directions, and if selvedge way, the material will resist the pulling, as the selvedge threads are strong and firm. *Weft* threads will give or stretch when pulled. Some materials will stretch as much as an inch or two in a yard. It is not wise to stretch the material to this extent, as it will be pulled out of shape for working purposes.

2. The selvedge threads are often coarser and more closely twisted than the weft, and in some materials stand out more prominently.

3. The selvedge threads are straight, whereas the weft threads seem to have an uneven, slightly wavy, crinkled appearance, caused by being passed over and under the warp in the process of manufacture. The weft threads are also much looser.

4. There is sometimes a difference in the sound if the material be pulled. The warp threads produce a sharp, shrill sound ; the weft threads are duller and heavier. This difference is not noticeable in common calicoes.

5. When material is torn, the frayings at the selvedge edge are often short and close ; at the weft edge the fringe is longer and more irregular in length (this is very noticeable in a good flannel).

6. Selvedge threads will not break unless pulled tightly, and a long length of selvedge thread can often be withdrawn,

but the weft threads have a tendency to break every few inches, even with the slightest strain.

When measuring length of material, the inch tape is applied to the selvedge way first, and to the weft edge afterwards, so that in stating the dimensions of a piece of material (*i.e.*, the length and the width) the *selvedge is always given first*, thus : 36 in. selvedge way and 18 in. weft way, would be read as—36 by 18 ; similarly, 2 in. selvedge way and 7 in. weft would be read as —2 by 7. It is most important that this be understood.

Selvedge way material is sometimes spoken of as " the right way of the stuff," and the weft way as " the wrong way." This is not a correct expression, as for some parts of a garment the weft way has to be cut and worked, and therefore the weft way is the " right way " for the purpose.

NOTE.—*All garments*, with the exception of a few severe fashions in dresses, are made up so that the *selvedge threads of the material run downwards*, that is from neck to feet, and from shoulder to wrist. This is important, as *portions* of garments are often asked for at examinations, and the right way of material upon which to represent the part must be the first consideration.

All bands, whether for neck, waist, wrist, or knee, are made with the selvedge running *round*, that is, at right angles to the other parts of the garments. Bands are made *selvedge way* in order that they may not stretch or split, which they would do if made with the weft way.

A yoke, which is merely a shaped band, follows the same rule, and the selvedge threads are usually placed across the back— exceptions are sometimes made with regard to shirt yokes and dresses.

It makes a great difference both in *appearance* and *wear* of a garment if it be cut the proper way of the stuff, and it is impossible to calculate the necessary quantity of material required for a garment, without taking into consideration the weft width.

Cutting-out paper is called " lined or extension " paper. It is whitey-brown, is tough, and has distinguishing red lines, ¼ in. apart, *which indicate the selvedge way of the material.* Every quarter yard is often marked with a different coloured line. Each whole sheet measures 45 or 46 in. by 36. It would be extravagant to use this paper for practice purposes in schools, as ordinary newspaper will answer for children's cutting out, unless for a special use. Tissue paper is too flimsy to be of much value ; besides, the size of the sheets is too small to be of any good but for the smallest garments.

Sectional paper is used for drawing diagrams. The paper is divided into small sections or squares, ¼ in. apart. Each small square represents *one* inch of the full-size pattern, and the drawing is said to be ¼ scale.

Scale means drawing in a fixed proportion to the actual size, by using one or more squares as the unit of measurement, and chequered paper is used to save unnecessary measuring.

The advantage of scale drawing is that it economizes space, and enables a large garment to be represented in a relatively small and convenient manner, so that measurements can be easily seen.

It is customary to letter (A, B, C, D, etc.) certain portions of a drawing (particularly corners, angles, and ends of lines), in order that each section of a diagram may be readily referred to.

The cost of sectional paper is 2s. 6d. a quire. The size of each sheet is 30 in. by 20 in., and every inch is ruled in darker ink.

Many school publishers stock small sectional exercise books which are most useful.

FINAL HINTS BEFORE AN EXAMINATION.

Provide yourself with all implements and materials necessary.

Carefully read through the test required, and at once plan out the allotted time, so that when the work is collected no portion of what was asked for remains unattempted ; this is important, as a certain number of marks is given for each portion of work ; and if a candidate neglect any part, marks cannot be granted for it, and so she becomes the sufferer by the omission. A few inches of any stitch are quite sufficient to obtain full marks, if well done.

Any cutting-out should always be dealt with first. If you are not familiar with the garment, cut what looks proportionate to the eye, rather than leave the work unattempted.

Next undertake any plain needlework, portioning the time for each piece required ; say, 5 min. for hemming ; 10 min. seaming ; 10 min. button-hole ; 5 min. tape ; and so on. Be very careful to fasten off all ends neatly, remembering that marks are given for general finish.

Devote the remaining time to writing any directions on the paper pattern as to making up, which you would recommend, so that the examiner may credit you with a common-sense arrangement of your work, *and always state all the full-size measurements of the various parts of the pattern, very neatly, and in a conspicuous place.*

Should a diagram be needed, be sure it is *accurate* and *neat*, both of which are important features, and that all dimensions are given.

If the hints given throughout this and the following chapters are borne carefully in mind, and accepted in the kindly spirit with which they are given, failure or even a low mark, at any needlework examination, will be an unknown occurrence.

CHAPTER II

PRELIMINARY STEPS IN TEACHING NEEDLEWORK

I. Introduction.—It is only by reducing work to method and system that teachers can cope with the difficulties that beset the path of instructing the young in plain needlework. Graduated teaching is most essential in every subject, but especially in an art which requires so much deftness, finger skill, and manipulation.

It has been agreed and proved beyond doubt that the best means of training the eye and the muscles of the hand to habits of exactness and neatness in needlework is by frequent and systematic practice in holding material and implements in a *correct* position. Simultaneous movements, which are framed to train raw children's fingers (if one may so speak of the unskilled) into habits of accuracy and precision, with regard to needlework, by means of the repetition of certain actions, are very essential to good class teaching.

Definite directions are of the greatest benefit where large numbers are concerned, and in the hands of a skilful teacher their value can never be over-estimated, as they form the foundation of all careful work.

The following graduated steps in teaching are usually adopted, and in order to ensure success, it is imperative that each step be thoroughly mastered before proceeding to the next one—

    I.   Needle threading.
   II. Proper position of thimble.
  III. Combining the use of needle and thimble.
  IV. Placing material on finger for hemming.
   V. The making of a stitch.

Before commencing to work, the teacher must exercise the class in showing right and left hands, in order to arrest the attention of her pupils, and to prepare them for prompt obedience to her commands. The class should be taught the names of the different fingers, and the children should have frequent practice in distinguishing one finger from another. [*Note.*—Since it is not considered expedient for children to begin needlework so young as in former years, this preliminary practice may be almost dispensed with, or reduced to a minimum.]

In *teaching*, each action must be fully and slowly explained, then when the class are familiar with each step, just the set phrase may be used.

A teacher's position during the lesson is *in front of her class·* No doubt there will be several backsliders, but it would be as well to give these little ones a lesson by themselves, than try to set them right individually, as by so doing the rest of the class may suffer. A large amount of patient labour, and untiring energy, are necessary to make little fingers produce the work required from them. Slow, steady, and repeated practice are the essentials to success. Ten minutes to a quarter of an hour is sufficient time to continue *an actual lesson in handling the material and implements,* but only a few minutes are necessary for a revision as an introduction to a needlework lesson.

STEP I.—NEEDLE THREADING.

Class Taught.—Whatever age children may be, whether they are in an Infants' school, and are taught to work when six years of age, or if older and in a Girls' school, these necessary preliminary steps should be worked. The time spent upon each stage will be considerably less than with younger infants.

Apparatus.—No. 5 sewing needle (ground downs) and Nos. 30 or 36 cotton are suitable, or a No. 4 needle and fine embroidery cotton. The teacher may use a large packing needle and fine string to demonstrate each step to the class.

NOTE.—The Nos. given below in the " Action of Children " are *not* to be taught as No. 1, 2, etc. ; they are merely numbered to show the stepwise processes in teaching, and are arranged in order of difficulty. Correct manipulation is *most* important with beginners. Bad habits are *very* troublesome to remedy.

No.	*Teacher's Directions.*	*Action of Children.*
1.	Pick up cotton.	Take up the cotton between the thumb and finger of the right hand, leaving a little piece showing.
2.	Point the end.	Sharpen the end with the left forefinger and thumb.
3.	Take up needle.	Take up the needle between the thumb and the first and second fingers of the left hand. Hold it with the eye upwards a little below the chin, and so that the eye can be seen above the first finger.
4.	Cotton to the eye.	Let the right-hand thumb *rest* upon the left thumb-nail, at the same time pointing the cotton to the eye of the needle.
5.	Pass it through.	Pass the thread through the eye—when just a little way in, take hold of the top of the needle with the right-hand thumb and finger.

No. Teacher's Directions.	Action of Children.
6. Catch hold cotton.	Catch the end of the cotton with the left hand, and draw through, making a long end and a short one.
7. Show threaded needles.	Hold the needle in the right hand, with ends hanging.

Remarks.—Some teachers prefer to use the left hand for the right, while demonstrating each step to a class. This plan is optional and, although it may serve to make the children use the hand they should do, nevertheless, the positions of the front and back of the teacher's hand are relatively wrongly placed ; besides, this left-handed working cannot be properly managed in teaching knitting.

If the teacher uses the same hand as the children, she must stand in such a position that the class can see every movement. The needle and thread should be held naturally—not with extended arms, or the children will imitate.

In the early stages, Nos. 1 and 2 must be practised several times, then No. 3 by itself, and afterwards 1, 2, and 3 in succession. Using both hands correctly is always a matter of difficulty for little children, as while the attention is fixed on one hand the other is quite forgotten. It is only the utmost patience, constant practice and kindly teaching which will overcome these weaknesses.

STEP II.—PROPER POSITION OF THIMBLE.

Apparatus.—Each child to be provided with a thimble, placed downwards upon the desk.

NOTE.—Besides the usual practice in showing right and left hands, the class should be able to readily distinguish the different fingers.

No. Teacher's Directions.	Action of Children.
1. Raise the right hand.	Hold the right hand so that the palm faces the chest. Spread out the fingers, pointing them to the left. About 4 to 5 in. from the chest is a convenient distance.
2. Take up thimble.	Put all the fingers of the left hand round the thimble.
3. Put it on finger.	Place the thimble on the middle or longest finger of the right hand.

No child should ever be allowed to make a stitch without using a thimble, and one that will fit properly.

STEP III.—COMBINING THE USE OF NEEDLE AND THIMBLE.

[The aim at this stage is : (1) To secure the eye of the needle being held firmly against the top of the thimble ; (2) to ensure the holding of the needle *very near the point* with the right-hand thumb and finger ; and (3) to allow the third and fourth fingers to be *thrown away* from the palm of the hand (this latter is most important, as freedom and speed with work can never be made unless the hand has sufficient play). Elder girls *very frequently* need reminding of the proper position of the needle in conjunction with the thimble.]

Apparatus.—Needle No. 5, coloured cotton No. 30 or 36, and a thimble for each child.

NOTE.—Teachers cannot be too particular in enforcing the proper use of thimble and needle. No child will ever become a skilful worker until it has a complete mastery over its tools ; and to teach the correct position of needle, thread, and thimble, *at the right time, viz., before material is used*, must be the aim of every teacher. By neglecting this step, progress is retarded and, worse still, bad habits are formed, which are most difficult to surmount, and good results are next to impossible.

No.	*Teacher's Directions.*	*Action of Children.*
1.	Take up needle.	Take up the threaded needle in the right-hand thumb and finger.— Point to left, eye to right.
2.	Put needle under thumb.	Hold *the point* of the needle just under the thumb-nail of the left hand.
3.	Thimble upon eye of needle.	Put the *top* of the thimble on the eye of the needle. (Any part of the top may be used, but the side next the forefinger is generally considered the most suitable.)
4.	Slip thumb and finger down the needle.	Slip the right-hand thumb and forefinger down the needle to meet the left thumb, and hold firmly.
5.	Raise needle.	Lift the needle up a little way, keeping the other fingers free, and the thimble still on the eye.
6.	Curve hand.	Bend the knuckles of the right hand a little towards the teacher.

Remarks.—As the class advance and the hands gain power over the needle, these detailed steps may be shortened ; but, at the present stage, no time will be wasted which is spent in perfecting the handling of the needle and the using of thimble.

STEP IV.—PLACING MATERIAL ON THE FINGER
FOR HEMMING.

Material Used.—Small strips of soft calico, with hems fixed (about ¼-in. wide).   Casement cloth is also very suitable.

Large coarse specimen for teacher.   A piece of sacking canvas, or Hessian, with a carpet needle and coloured thread, or a sail needle and very thick wool, will prove of excellent service.

Note.—From time to time as children use material, the opportunity will be favourable for lessons bearing upon the same, also the other implements which have been used. Attention should be drawn to the fixed hem, and its use explained, the position in which the work should be placed on the desk, viz., with the fold of the hem upwards, distinguishing the right side from the wrong.

No.	Teacher's Directions.	Action of Children.
1.	Take hold of work.	Take hold of the work with the thumb and finger of the right hand, at the top right-hand corner.
2	Bend the left hand.	Bend the left hand towards the chest, placing the ball of the thumb midway on the cushion of the left forefinger, and bending the *second joint.*
3	Place work on finger and hold firmly.	Raise the left thumb, and place the right-hand end of work over the first joint of left forefinger, so that the edge to be hemmed lies just *above the bed of the nail* of finger, and the thumb-nail *half-way* across the edge of the hem. Hold firmly in place with the second finger.

Remarks.—For little children it is advisable to hold the work over *one* finger, but as the muscles are developed it can be placed over two fingers if preferred.

The elbows must not rest on the hips, but be kept easily away from the side in an unconstrained position.

Note.—It is most important that all work is held at "the correct working distance" from the eyes, viz., 10 in. (12 if possible). Children must be made to understand that they should sit upright while at work, and keep the material at the proper distance.

STEP V.—MAKING A STITCH.

Apparatus.—Strips of material with hems fixed, and about five or six stitches worked, the threaded needle being placed in position for making another stitch, just a little way in ; thimbles ; a coarse specimen for the teacher. (Half a yard of cotton is sufficiently long for the children's use.)

NOTE.—Some teachers prefer *teaching* this step with the thread unfastened. This plan has advantages, as the cotton is not so likely to get knotted, but the *slope* and *size* of the stitches already worked give a correct idea of what has to be imitated, and in a few lessons the pupils will be capable of commencing.

It is supposed that the class are able to place the work in position, and hold the needle in the thimble properly, before commencing the making of a stitch.

Class-notice.—Needle (1) **IN,** on the single material—just touching the hem ; (2) **OUT**—up on the hem ; (3) piece of material **ON** the needle.

No.	*Teacher's Directions.*	*Action of Children.*
1.	Place work.	Put the hem in position on the forefinger and so that the point of needle is under left thumb-nail.
2.	Thimble on needle.	These movements are fully described in Step III, but as the class are more advanced fewer directions are needed.
3.	Take hold and draw out.	
4.	Make a stitch.	This must be well in front of the cotton, and the needle only put in a little way, pointing to the middle of the thumb-nail. (For a first stitch, the holes which the needle made will be a guide.)
5.	Move thumb.	Keep the fingers still, and bring the right-hand thumb over beside the left one (the thumbs should form almost a right angle). Press firmly.

No.	Teacher's Directions.	Action of Children.
6.	Push needle in.	The thimble must push the needle through, almost up to the eye.
7.	Catch hold of needle.	Take hold of the needle between the thumb and forefinger, keeping the thimble finger up, and draw the cotton out a little way.
8.	Draw out.	Close the thimble finger over the cotton and draw out over the third finger towards the right-hand shoulder. The cotton is sometimes brought out *under* the third finger. The former plan is preferred.

Remarks.—In the early lessons it is advisable that the class should be told at each step what is to be done. Each individual teacher can frame words suitable for her pupils, *e.g.*—

1. Place the work over the finger.
2. Put the thimble on the eye of the needle.
3. Take hold of the needle near the point.
4. Make a stitch.
5. Move the thumb. } These are *most* important steps.
6. Push the needle in.
7. Catch hold of the needle.
8. Close down the thimble finger over the cotton, and draw up over the shoulder. Repeat from No. **4.**

When some practice has been given the definite direction may be used to start the class, and then the pupils may work alone.

Needlework is not compulsory for children under seven years of age. Every teacher who knows the value of early finger training, will use all her energy to perfect her pupils in the foregoing steps, not merely because children are required to hem, and that it would be impossible to teach this individually—but for the reason, that all definite instruction helps to secure prompt obedience to commands, exactness in detail, cultivates the faculty of observation, exercises the children's imitative abilities, trains the muscles, and without this initiatory instruction to obtain the correct handling of implements and material, a child will never become a quick or skilful worker.

The above suggestions only give an outline of what may be done with a class of children towards laying a good foundation. Each teacher should study her subject well, before attempting to demonstrate to her class, as one is often tempted to neglect preparation for anything which seems so simple ; and yet it is the simplicity (to the teacher) which adds to the difficulty of teaching. These directions are prepared for those teachers who have not hitherto had occasion to study the subject in detail, and are written, not as hard and fast rules, but merely *as a guide*, to be *increased* or *decreased* at the discretion of the teacher, to suit the wants of her pupils, or any special circumstances attending the organisation of the school. It must be borne in mind that these preliminary steps are the foundation of all successful teaching in needlework, and the teacher should remember that the training the children receive in this branch of work, although it may seem wearisome, will bear fruit later on, and infinitely repay for the trouble and time expended.

Note.—It is not expected that children at this stage of proficiency are to fix hems; but as soon as the stitches can be formed, the class should be taught to fix and tack a hem, and commence the work. (*See* p. 20 : Headings IV to VI.)

Soft calico or casement cloth is the most suitable material for beginners. Supposing after several lessons only half a class are able to fix a hem nicely, these few pupils will be all the better for having acquired this finger skill, and the teacher will have the satisfaction of knowing that, besides saving her own time, she has begun to sow the seeds of " self-help " in her little pupils —a quality which adds so considerably to the happiness, well-being, and comfort of every individual.

Children must *not* be allowed to do as they please in the matter of holding their implements with the hope that eventually the best way will suggest itself to the child's mind. Such a theory, which for a time was advocated by some exponents of Handwork, has almost passed, and the value of *systematic* teaching and supervision has proved to be a most essential part of a training in Needlework. The advantage of these " stepwise processes " (called in bygone times, " drills ") cannot be over-rated, as they are the pivot on which the *entire* success of the subject turns.

CHAPTER III

HEMMING

I. Introduction.—Before commencing to hem, it is *very essential* that the student should carefully study the preceding chapter (particularly Steps III, IV, and V), which will ensure that the material and implements used are held in such a manner as to produce good hemming ; in fact, it is quite impossible to work freely and well, unless attention be given to these elementary details, which are the foundation of all good work.

The Note at the upper part of page 16 should be carefully read here, and its principle carried out in *all* needlework. Although hemming is considered an elementary stitch, it is one of the most difficult to work correctly.

II. Definition of a Hem.—A hem is a fold of material, turned down and folded over so as to protect a raw edge, and also to make a firm, neat border, to any household linen or article of clothing.

III. Preparation of the Material.—Hems are worked both selvedge and weft way of the material, according to that part of the garment upon which the hem is needed. Material is easier for children to *turn* if torn selvedge way, but the *stitches* show to better effect if the material is the weft way of the stuff. The first turn must *not* be deep ; for narrow hems, such as would be put at the edge of frills, the first turn should be nearly, if not quite, as deep as the second ; transparent material should have as much turned the first time as is needed for the depth of the hem ; $\frac{1}{8}$ to $\frac{1}{4}$ in. is ample for a *first* turning on all material, unless it is very thick and likely to fray. A deep turn does not give strength, it only adds bulkiness and makes the hem clumsy. Inexperienced workers invariably put deep turnings.

If turning material selvedge way, the fold can be kept straight by passing the middle finger of the left hand at the back of the material, after the thumb and finger have made the turn ; if folding a curve, or weft way material, it is better to pleat the material under the right thumb. Hems should be of the same depth throughout. A small piece of paper or card, if cut the necessary depth, is an assistance in securing regularity if a deep hem is required, and in thick materials it is advisable to tack the *first* turn as well as the second, and also the top of the fold.

Excellent practice is given by hemming round a curve, as for the bottom of a shirt, fancy pinafore or apron, armhole, neck, sash ends, etc., care is needed in fixing—if a *concave* curve, the hem will probably need stretching to make it set flatly ; if *convex*, the turning must be eased or puckering will result. A hem will set nicely round a convex curve if small triangular folds of material be snipped out from the *first* fold.

19

If it is necessary to turn a square or oblong of material, both the selvedge or *opposite* sides should be turned first, and then the weft edges.

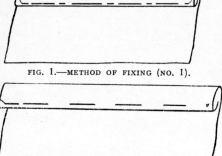

FIG. 1.—METHOD OF FIXING (NO. 1).

FIG. 2.—METHOD OF FIXING (NO. 2).

IV. Method of Fixing. —All tacking threads should be near the edge of the hem ; a long stitch (say, ½ in.) and a short one alternating will be found more successful than continuous long stitches. (Fig. 1.) This method of tacking is excellent upon all thick materials.

Very little children should be taught to make a neat tidy knot for securing the cotton and to tack with all stitches the same length until some progress is made. (Fig. 2.) Hems of ¼-in. in depth should be chosen for the early lessons. A *very* narrow hem is as difficult to fix as a very wide one.

V. Position of the Work.—Whatever width the hem may be, the edge of it should be placed just above the *bed* of the nail of the left forefinger, and held in position by keeping the *middle* of the left thumb on the edge of the hem. Many persons prefer placing the work over *two* fingers, but as this requires greater muscular power, over one finger is better for children's work. Fig. 3 shows the work over two fingers.

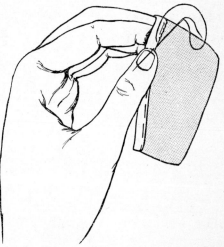

FIG. 3.—POSITION OF THE WORK IN THE HAND.

VI. Commencement of the Stitch.—Point the needle away from the chest—catch only the upper fold—draw through till nearly ½ in. of cotton remains (a finger-nail length to a child)—tuck the end under the hem, using the needle for the purpose—hold the thumb firmly upon the hem and proceed with the work.

VII. Shape of the Stitch.—The stitch roughly forms a triangle, one side of which is seen on the right side of the material, and one side on the wrong, the base of the triangle extending from the lower part of one stitch to the lower part of the next. The point where the needle comes out on the hem should be *midway above the base*. The stitch is the diagonal of an oblong, so that, bearing this in mind, any number of stitches can be made to an inch, and yet correct in shape.

The hemming stitch is shown in Fig. 4. When making a stitch, the needle should point to the *middle* of the left thumb-nail, which will produce the slanting stitch shown in diagram, making an angle of about 30° with the edge of the hem.

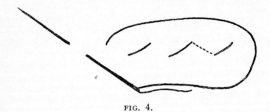

FIG. 4.

The size of the stitch and the number worked to an inch should vary according to the age and progress of the worker and the material used for practice, but fine needlework must not be allowed.

It is advisable to encourage little children to make *bold* stitches, say about six to an inch in the early stages ; and as skill and speed are gained, the stitches should be made somewhat smaller, so that by the time a fair state of proficiency is reached, about ten or twelve stitches to an inch will be found a good average number for ordinary practical work.

It is not intended that stitches should be counted, as the idea is merely to secure a standard of uniformity, and needs keeping more in the spirit than the letter ; but all hemming stitches should show through so plainly on the right side that they might easily be numbered if desired.

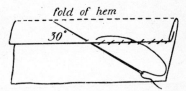

FIG. 5.—HEMMING IN PROGRESS.

The needle should, as it were, *scoop* up the material, and not skim over it. Hemming needs a peculiar position of the hand in order to produce a stitch which is *well taken through* and yet regular. The hand must be poised so that more of the back part of the hand is seen when putting in the needle than is usual for other stitches, so as to enable the needle to dig up the material, in fact, the point of the needle should be put in almost vertically, and then the back of the hand turned from the worker while the stitch is taken up.

If the stitch be worked as described above, a wide open V-shaped stitch will be produced, and in order to work quickly it is necessary to make the stitch so. It has a prettier appearance, and is decidedly more practical than the upright hemming, which is now taught but rarely, and hardly ever with good results, as it always appears such laboured work.

VIII. Joins in the Cotton.—Cut the cotton off, leaving rather less than half an inch, slightly raise the hem, put the needle under the fold, unpick half a stitch, and *leave the end hanging*, the little hole where the cotton was unpicked being ready to receive the needle with the new cotton. If the thread breaks (and children must snap the cotton sharply), $1\frac{1}{2}$, $2\frac{1}{2}$, or even $3\frac{1}{2}$ stitches must be unpicked, till an end sufficiently long is obtained. Breaking the thread causes the material to pucker a little, but it must be straightened with the thumb and finger *before the stitches are unpicked*. Commence with the new cotton, catching only the upper fold, draw it through till it is the same length as

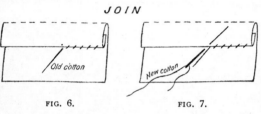

JOIN

FIG. 6.   FIG. 7.

the other end, give the two ends a *little twist together* with the right hand thumb and forefinger, and then tuck the twist under the hem. This makes the join most secure, and will result in two perfect stitches, the one old and the other new, appearing at regular distances on the right side. (*See* Figs. 6 and 7.)

IX. Finishing Off.—The usual plan is to make another stitch over the last one, and then slip the needle up to the top of the fold before breaking the thread, or in the case of a narrow hem some distance along the fold. (Fig. 8.)

When hemming over a thickness, such as a seam or another hem, put the stitches a little closer than usual, but do not attempt to take the needle deep. The work will be quite strong if only the top part of the lower thickness be caught ; besides, the needle is less likely to break.

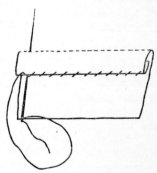

FIG. 8.—FINISHING OFF HEMMING.

X. Depths of Hems Suitable for Different Purposes.

Article.				Width of Hem.
Edges of Frills	.	.	.	$\frac{1}{4}$ inch.
Openings in Garments	.	.	.	$\frac{1}{8}$,,

Article.	Width of Hem.
Pocket Handkerchiefs (for children's work, a wide hem looks well) .	$\frac{1}{6}$ to $\frac{3}{4}$ inch
Bottoms of Shirts	$\frac{1}{4}$,,
Ends of Sheets, Tablecloths, Towels, and Kitchen Cloths	$\frac{3}{8}$,, 1 ,,
Backs of Children's Frocks . .	$\frac{3}{4}$,, 1 ,,
Bottoms of Children's Chemises .	$\frac{1}{2}$,, 1 ,,
,, Nightdresses . .	$\frac{3}{4}$,, 1 ,,
,, Drawers . .	$\frac{3}{4}$,, $1\frac{1}{4}$,,
,, Pinafores and Aprons .	1 ,, $1\frac{1}{2}$,,
,, Frocks . . .	$1\frac{1}{2}$,, 2 ,,
Tops of Pillow-cases . . .	$1\frac{1}{2}$,, $2\frac{1}{2}$,,

XI. Faults met with in hemming are—

1. *Upright stitches*, caused by putting the needle in almost underneath where the cotton came out instead of advancing a little distance onward. Also by putting the needle in perpendicularly instead of *pointing it to the middle of the left thumb nail*.

2. *Split* hemming (the worst fault), caused by not taking the needle through clearly to the right side, but letting it skim the threads, and consequently, with the least wear, the stitch gives way.

This may be overcome by following out the directions given under Heading VII.

3. *Single thread* hemming is not often seen now, since fine work has been so condemned.

4. *Straight* hemming is made by putting the needle in horizontally as for running, instead of in an oblique direction.

5. *Stitches too small* (a very common fault) and badly proportioned.

6. Commencement—joins—finish—insecure, inaccurate, or clumsy.

7. Hem not turned evenly, and badly fixed.

8. Material puckered (cotton pulled too tightly).

To ensure good hemming—

I. **Make every Stitch show through clearly on the right side.**

II. Let **all stitches** be uniform in size (threads are not to be studied, but even distances gauged with the eye). Ten to twelve stitches to an inch are a suitable number for students, if using materials of medium texture.

III. Make *every* stitch accurate in shape.

IV. Let the commencement—joins—and finish be strong and neat.

V. Be sure that the material is well flattened when the work is completed.

CHAPTER IV

SEWING

I. Its Use and Application.—This stitch is sometimes called " top sewing," and is used for joining two pieces of material together, when the raw edges have been turned in, as in securing the end of a band. It is also applied to selvedges, when it is necessary that they should be sewn together for the purpose of making material wider ; selvedges are joined in making a pillow-case, or in putting on gores. Children should not be taught to sew by using selvedges, as they are generally uneven and harsh. Sewing is one of the strongest stitches used in plain needlework. It should be worked upon the *right side* as a rule. The edges to be sewn must always be placed exactly together, and firmly tacked. No stitch so well repays for careful fixing.

II. Preparation of Material.—Sewing should be taught on small strips of material torn *selvedge* way or cut on the selvedge slant. The edges of the material should be turned once only on to the *wrong* side, faced together, and securely fixed. The needle should be passed through the material almost vertically in fixing, so that the material which is uppermost sets *quite flatly* against that which rests on the forefinger.

III. Position of the Hands and the Method of Holding the Work. —The left hand should be held about 5 or 6 inches in front of the chest. The right elbow must be kept slightly away from the side, and the right hand (particularly the wrist) curved towards the chest, and always *at the back of the left hand*. The success of the work will entirely depend upon the way in which it is held. Sewing is worked from *right to left*, therefore as much of the material to be sewn as can be conveniently arranged should be held loosely in the fork of the left hand, which is formed by the thumb and forefinger. This will prevent the work from dragging. (There is a tendency to work backwards, viz. from left to right, which is accounted for by the ease with which the material is handled in this way.)

Imagine the first joint of the left forefinger divided perpendicularly into three equal parts. Place the beginning of the portion to be sewn at the upper edge of the finger, leaving one-third of the finger free. Hold the material in place by the left thumb, which should be *midway* between the first joint and the tip of the forefinger.

The diagram (Fig. 9) shows the first joint of the left forefinger ; XI the position of the material in starting. The distance from

24

X1 to X2 will be about the amount sewn, before it becomes necessary to move the work round the finger. The part of the fore-

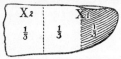

FIG. 9.—FIRST JOINT OF FOREFINGER.

finger which is shaded in Fig. 9 should always be to the *right* of the needle in working. The middle finger will be ready to hold in place the completed work. The material should only be moved so that the stitch at X2 is placed at X1, and the needle should be left *in the work*, as if about to make another stitch, while the position of the work is changed. By this guide, the ugly " break " in the regularity of sewing, which is caused by moving the material too far round the finger, is avoided. Great care must be taken that the sewing is held *round* the finger and not *over* the nail, or puckering is certain. (Fig. 10.)

IV. Commencement. —Catch up just the extreme edge of the fold nearest the thumb, pointing the needle to the worker ; draw through till rather less than half an inch of cotton remains ; place this end *along the top* of the fold from right to left, using the needle for the purpose. (Fig. 11 shows an exaggerated appearance of the commencement of sewing if the seam were flattened out.) For beginners, it is

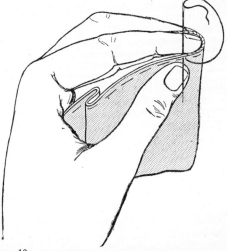

FIG. 10.—POSITION OF THE WORK ROUND THE FINGER.

The artist has drawn the material which is round the first finger a little too low ; it would be better if nearer the nail and covering up rather more of the first finger.

perhaps better that this little end be held down by putting the second finger over the first, and holding the end until a few stitches are worked (being careful to put the needle at the back of the cotton), by this time the end will keep firmly in place on the top of the seam.

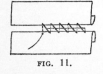

FIG. 11.

V. Shape of the Stitch.—This consists of an oblique thread from right to left on the right side, and a straight one joining the two edges on the wrong, producing a succession of printed Ns.

Fig. 12 shows the shape of the stitch. The dotted part of the stitch will be seen on the wrong side, when the work is flattened.

26

The needle must be inserted exactly at an angle of 90° with the work, so as to point *straight to the chest*. Any angle less than this will cause a larger amount of material to be taken between each stitch on the front side than the back, and, though only a trifle, will produce a pucker. Just the *extreme* edges of the fold must be taken up, or a harsh, clumsy ridge will result, which it will be next to impossible to flatten.

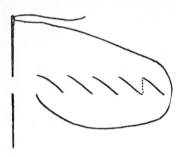

FIG. 12.—SEWING STITCH.

Cotton frequently becomes knotted in sewing because the wrong end is threaded. As the cotton is broken from the reel it seems natural to thread this end, because it is in the hand. Cotton may be likened to the stem of a tree, and the little hairy fibres (quite visible to the naked eye) to the branches, which if bent backwards would break. The same thing may be applied to the cotton. If *the end be threaded as it comes from the reel* the fibres will be rubbed smoothly in working, and will be less likely to become entangled. Children work with too long a length of cotton—24 in. to 26 in. is ample.

VI. Joins.—Cut the cotton, leaving about three-eighths of an inch. Insert the needle in the groove, and unpick the straight bar, or half-stitch, which will bring the cotton out between the folds. If the thread should break off close (and for children, who are not always provided with scissors, it is necessary to break the cotton), *straighten the work* between the thumb and finger of each hand, and unpick $2\frac{1}{2}$ or $3\frac{1}{2}$ stitches ; then proceed as for commencement, the little hole where the last stitch was unpicked being ready to receive the new cotton. Both old and new ends can then be laid on the *top* of the fold, and *sewn over* as the work goes on, as by this means two perfect stitches, the one old and the other new, are side by side. A teacher should illustrate the method of joining on a large coarse specimen (Hessian or sacking will answer the purpose) and two coloured wools. It is advisable when giving a first lesson on a join, that the cotton should be *cut* off the required length (the teacher should do this), as unpicking only the $\frac{1}{2}$ *stitch* will present less difficulty. Then in a subsequent lesson breaking the cotton may be introduced.

A neat finish is made by sewing back for 3 or 4 stitches, producing little crosses, or turning the work round, bringing the needle through to what is now the front side, and sewing from right to left, which is equally as strong, and makes double stitches. In fastening up the ends of a band, when the corner is reached, the needle must be slipped *between* the folds and the cotton cut off. This method is much neater and stronger than breaking the thread close. Figs. 13, 14, and 15 illustrate the join and finish. The small sketches are shown with the seam flattened out in order to make the method clearer.

VII. Flattening.—Sewing is not completed until the work is *well flattened*. First remove the tacking threads. Various implements are used for this purpose ; bone flatteners can be bought,

FINISH

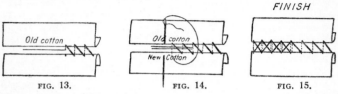

| FIG. 13. | FIG. 14. | FIG. 15. |

similar to a toothbrush handle ; the thimble is often used ; but nothing does as successfully as the thumb-nail of the left hand— the means which Nature provides.

SEAMING.

I. Definition.—Seaming, *i.e.*, sewing in combination with a fell ·(often called " a sew and fell seam "), is the method used to join two pieces of material with raw edges, when both right and wrong sides require to be made neat.

II. Preparation for Seaming.—Two pieces of material are necessary. For class-teaching children may be taught the preparation for a seam on strips of paper. Extension or lined paper, such as is used for cutting-out, is admirable for the purpose. It is tough, and the lines indicate right and wrong side, and also guide the turning. For practice purposes, material should be selvedge way, as the appearance of the work is so much better when done, and seams are generally this way in garments. Material on the selvedge slant or the curve has invariably to be seamed in a garment. It is essential that practice should be given in this work, as soon as familiarity is gained with the straight threads.

To prepare—turn down a narrow fold nearly one-sixth inch upon the wrong side of one piece ; fold the same depth on the right side of the second piece ; face the material entirely round, and fold over this last turn rather deeper than the first, so that the *raw* edge quite clears the folded edge. (Figs. 16 and 17.) A rule often given for a fell is, that the first turn should be two-thirds of the depth the fell is required to be when complete. Seams should always be narrow ($\frac{1}{4}$ in. or under, according

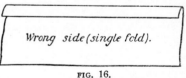

FIG. 16.

to the texture of the material), but must be perfectly flat.

Place the two wrong sides of the material together and tack holding the double fold to the worker, and keeping the left thumb and finger firmly on the seam while the needle is put in for tacking. It is better to stab the needle through the material for the first two or three stitches of tacking, the edges are not then so likely to slip out of place. The work is now ready for sewing, and when this is completed the fixing thread should be removed and the seam flattened for felling.

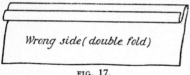

Wrong side (double fold)

FIG. 17.

III. Felling.—The edge on the wrong side is neatened by a fold of the material being hemmed down to cover the raw edges. This fold is called a " fell," and is so named because one piece of material is " struck " or " flattened " on to another. This stitch is *exactly* the same as hemming, only the material is more cumbersome to manage in the hand — hence the reason why the stitches are often so much more irregular and badly shaped than for hemming, which is always worked at the *edge* of some part of a garment, while felling generally comes *between* two pieces of material, and is, as a rule, accompanied by another stitch, viz., sewing or running.

When working on a small section,

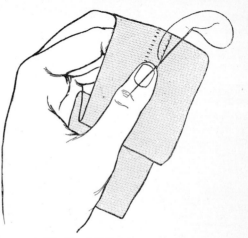

FIG. 18.—FELLING IN PROGRESS.

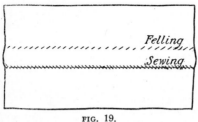

Felling

Sewing

FIG. 19.

gather up a portion of material in the fork formed by the thumb and finger of the left hand. This prevents dragging, and illustrates what must of necessity occur in a garment. (Fig. 18.)

Fig. 19 shows the seam complete.

IV. Application of Seams on Garments.—In the majority of garments, seams are in pairs, viz. for right and left side, and the fells must in consequence face each other. This is effected by starting *the turning* (not the fixing) in a reverse direction for opposite sides, thus—

Nightgowns. Commence the *right*-hand seam from the armhole, and the *left*-hand from the hem at the bottom.

Knickers and Combinations. Turn down the *right* leg from the knee, and the *left* leg from the seat.

Sleeves. Begin the *right* sleeve from the wrist, and the *left* from the armhole.

This process is called "pairing seams."

Each student is advised to practise this. It is a detail, but these little points make all the difference between a well-arranged garment and a poor one, and it is most important that in the making of underclothing the sewing of one portion should be arranged to match the sewing of the other portion, and similarly felling and felling, *e.g.*, the sewing of the *right sleeve* should match the sewing of the *right-hand seam* of the garment; also the sewing in the *left leg* of drawers should touch the sewing in the *right leg* when made into a pair, and so on with other garments.

For sleeves, where one piece of stuff is on the straight, and the other on the oblique or slant, always make the double turn on the straight side, as the seam is less likely to become stretched or puckered. The oblique side must be placed to the under part of the arm when the sleeve is inserted, and should be held towards the worker while the seam is sewn.

It is essentially a teacher's duty to look after the correct arrangement in the pairing of seams, which is rarely understood even by elder girls, and frequently proves a stumbling-block to young teachers, until they have had some experience in the management of class work.

V. Faults met with in Seaming are—

1. Uneven turnings, or too deep for the texture of the material.

2. Badly shaped and irregular stitches—

(*a*) Too close together.

(*b*) Taken too deeply below the edges and forming a harsh ridge which it is impossible to flatten.

3. Puckered sewing—caused by pulling the cotton too tightly or inserting the needle at some other angle than *straight to the chest*. Puckering is easily avoided if the directions for holding the work and the needle are carefully carried out.

4. Commencement — joins — finish — insecure, inaccurately worked, or clumsy in appearance.

5. Seam not flattened—this is most essential.

VI. Note.—(*a*) Sheets and towels and other articles of house-linen are often fixed as for hemming, and then the hem is turned back and the edges are sewn. This is called "a seamed hem," and is a very strong and neat method.

(*b*) When sewing up the corners of a hem, the *right* side must always face the worker while *both* the corners are sewn. The cotton which is used for the first corner should continue the hemming, and the second corner should be completed without making a fastening near the end.

CHAPTER V

PREPARATION OF A BAND

I. Definition.—A band is a small portion of material put on to a larger and fuller piece of material. It is used to hold the fullness together, to strengthen the edges, and to make parts of a garment more comfortable in wearing.

II. Preparation of Material.—Before children are taught to prepare bands it is very essential that an object lesson be given on the manufacture of material, so that the expression " selvedge and weft " (which should be as familiar as " bread and butter ") is to a large extent understood. (*See* pp. 7 and 8 for a full description of these threads.)

All bands should be torn so that the length of the band is the selvedge way of the material. The width of the band will depend upon the part of the garment for which the band is intended.

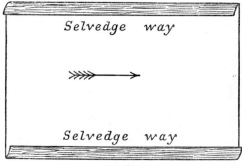

FIG. 20.

Small pieces of material, say 5 in. by 3 in., are sufficiently large for practice.

The selvedge edge should always be removed, as it is rarely even, and is very apt to cause the band to pucker.

The following graduated steps are necessary in making a band, and not one of them can be omitted in order to produce a successful piece of work—

1. The material for the band will probably have been torn, and this has a tendency to twist it ; therefore it is advisable to pull the material diagonally to straighten it, *before* any turning is done, so that it may set flatly when folded together.

2. Turn the *selvedge sides of the band first* and fold under *rather less* than ¼ in. This fold must be *exactly* by a thread, and the material stretched with the middle finger of the left hand. (Fig. 20.)

30

(It is with bated breath that we speak of working stitches by threads, and it should be deprecated as much as possible, but it is essential to the neat appearance of a band that it is *turned* by a thread.)

3. Turn the weft edges similarly, pleating the fold between the thumb and finger to prevent stretching, and *keeping the corners quite to a right angle.* (Fig. 21.)

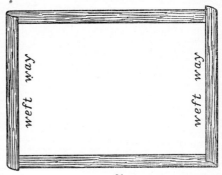

FIG. 21.

4. Fold the long selvedge sides together, holding the corners in the hands and again pulling the band to straighten it. (Fig. 22.)

5. Tack the band on the right side all round the turned down edges so as to keep the band flat.

The stitches should be about ⅜ in. in length and *perfectly* straight, and the needle must stab

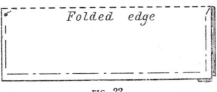

Folded edge

FIG. 22.

through the corners while the material is held firmly between the left thumb and forefinger. If the band is intended for a garment, the *weft* edges only will need tacking.

III. Faults likely to occur are—

1. Band fixed with the selvedge threads running the *depth* of the band instead of along the *length.*

2. Band not fixed evenly by a thread.

3. Turnings too deep. This can be easily detected by holding the work to the light.

4. *Opposite* edges not turned in succession.

5. Corners not at right angles.

6. Raw edges showing.

7. Irregular tacking.

8. A twisted appearance caused by insufficient pulling.

IV. Remarks.—The preparation of a band is a most difficult piece of work even for experienced workers. It is a sure test of good teaching if the band is well prepared.

CHAPTER VI

SETTING ON TAPES

(FOR BANDS AND TOWELS, ETC.)

I. Introduction.—This process should be taught to girls who are able to make a neat band. There are several methods of securing a tape to a band. The teacher should select one plan and definitely teach it, and not try to combine two or three ways in the course of a short time, unless she has exceptionally skilful pupils.

The lesson should be demonstrated by the teacher using a large piece of paper prepared as for a band, and a strip of contrasting paper to represent a string ; or a band of *coarse* towelling and *wide* tape or common ribbon. By means of this apparatus and blackboard illustrations it is possible to obtain good results.

Linen tape should be used for all good work, although a common make is often chosen for practice purposes.

II. Use of Tape Strings—

1. Strings are used for the purpose of tying together certain loose parts of clothing, or house linen, for comfort and neatness (*e.g.*, aprons, pinafores, frocks, drawers, pillowcases, etc.).

2. Loops of tape are frequently put upon towels, as a provision for hanging them upon a hook.

III. Position of Tape Strings—

1. When put upon a band, intended just to meet, the tapes should both be sewn to the edge of a band. If the band is meant to overlap, as for a pinafore, apron, or drawers, the right-hand tape will be put on the under or wrong side of band at the edge, and the left-hand tape on the upper or right side of band, at a convenient distance from the edge. (*See* Fig. 26.)

2. Bands sometimes have a loop of tape, if a tape string is required to pass through the loop.

3. Towels usually have the loop of tape at the corner, or at the middle of one side.

4. A barracoat, or infant's long flannel, should have one set of tapes at the edge of the skirt, and the corresponding set several inches from the edge on the right side.

5. For pillow-cases, the tapes are placed quite an inch from the edge of the hem.

IV. Rules which may be Applied to all Methods of Putting on Tapes—

1. The tape must be attached to the garment in such a position as to fulfil the purpose for which it is intended, whether this may be for tying, strengthening, or neatening.

2. If tapes are attached to bands, it is usual for the width of the tape to regulate the depth which is to be secured, so that the attachment may form a square of stitches on the material. Very wide tape may form an oblong.

3. The stitches must be strong and well-shaped. Sewing and felling may be used, stitching and felling, or stitching alone. There is a tendency to make upright and irregular stitches in the felling, which is accounted for by the awkwardness in handling. *Felling should never be used on the right side.* Every stitch must show through clearly on the reverse

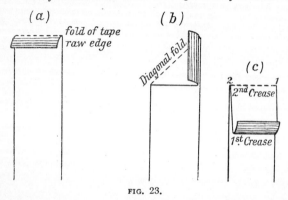

FIG. 23.

side if possible, but, if the material is very thick, it is difficult to take the stitches through; but uniformity must be maintained.

4. The ends of narrow tape should be button-holed, and wide tape is usually hemmed.

5. The finished appearance of the tape should be symmetrical, and perfectly flat, and strength and neatness its principal features.

V. Different Ways of Securing Tape to Material.—The method described is suitable for young pupils. It is presumed that each child has a band, upon which to sew the tape at the end (*not at right angles to the folded edge of the band*). This increases the difficulty of putting on, but it must be mastered, as it so often occurs. It is needless to remark that there should be no raw edges anywhere upon the band, and the ends of the band may be sewn up as for a garment if desired, but this is not advisable for beginners, and may be chosen later on.

Preparation of Tape.—Commence by turning down a narrow

fold, say, one-eighth of an inch (" *a* " in diagram); turn the tape round so that the raw edge faces *away* from the worker ; fold over the top left-hand corner, till it is exactly below the top right-hand corner ; this forms the diagonal of a square (" *b* " in diagram) ; raise this fold and make another crease, perfectly straight from the corner of the diagonal, across the width of the tape (" *c* " in diagram). The tape is now folded as for a sew and fell. (Fig. 23.)

The square for *all* tapes should be prepared in this way, and excellent practice is given by turning a strip of paper preparatory to the tape.

To Secure the Tape to the Band.—Hold the band so that right side faces worker. (Fig. 24.) Place the raw edge of the tape (that is, the turned square) to the wrong side of the band, keeping the crease which was folded last (2nd crease—1, 2) even with

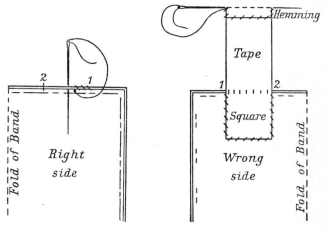

FIG. 24.—RIGHT SIDE OF BAND SHOW- ING POSITION OF TAPE AT EDGE.

FIG. 25.—WRONG SIDE OF BAND SHOW- ING POSITION OF TAPE WHEN COMPLETE.

the edges of the band and in the middle of the depth. Hold firmly between the thumb and finger. Three edges are seen— two of the band and one of the tape. If the material is soft, the three edges may be sewn, but the fold nearest the worker and the fold of the tape must be caught. Begin to sew at the right-hand corner of the tape. Do not break off the cotton when the tape is secured. Lift up the long end of the tape, and a little square will be seen on the wrong side in readiness for felling around three of its sides. (Fig. 25.) No fixing is necessary. Flatten the sewing. It is a good plan for a teacher to gauge the number of stitches that may be put in each side, and tell her pupils. This may seem a detail, but secures uniformity, and may be dispensed with as proficiency is gained. To finish off, slip the needle between the material and the tape.

The end of tape must be turned for a narrow hem, so that the hemming stitches may come on the same side as the felling. The sides of this little fold must be sewn ; the number of stitches needed may again be a useful guide to a child. Guard against upright stitches in this tiny piece of hemming. It is a difficulty for little fingers to manage so small a hem—hence the error in the shape of the stitch. When the second side is sewn up, slip the needle *along the hem* before breaking the cotton, and flatten the hem thoroughly. (Fig. 25.)

A result similar to the above is produced by preparing the tape as described, but instead of placing the raw edge of the tape to the wrong side of the band, keep the tape on the *right* side with the *raw* edge of the square facing worker, and sew and fell as explained above.

Children should be practised in putting on tapes of various widths.

The ends of narrow tapes should be button-holed. This will prevent them curling up or fraying. A neat commencement is made by running the needle parallel with the edge, and working the button-hole stitch over the cotton. Finish off similarly.

A Tape on the Right Side of the Band.—The tape is prepared as in Fig. 23, but opened flat so that only the raw edge is turned in.

The tape is placed at a distance in from the edge of the band and must be *stitched* on the *right* side to form a square. (Fig. 26.)

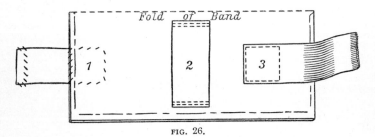

FIG. 26.

A Stitched Loop of Tape.—The tape should not be cut *less* than $1\frac{3}{4}$ in. The ends are turned in *once*. The tape is placed on the right side of the garment and stitched with two rows of stitching, the second row securing the raw edges of the tape.

Fig. 26 shows a tacked band with three tapes—

1. Sewn to the edge and felled on the *wrong* side.
2. A stitched loop.
3. Stitched on the *right* side at a distance from the edge to accommodate the overlapping of the band.

A Tape for a Pillow-case.—The hem on a pillow-case should be from $1\frac{1}{2}$ to 2 in. deep and the tape about $\frac{5}{8}$ in. in width.

1. Prepare the tape with a square as shown in Fig. 23, but open it out *quite flat*, so that only the creases show.

2. Place the tape, quite straight, on the wrong side, with the first crease about $\frac{1}{4}$ in. from the hemming stitches, or so that it just clears the turned-in edge. Pin or tack in position. (Fig. 27.)

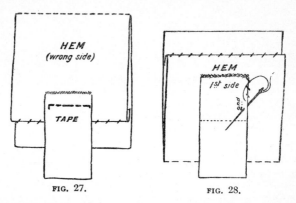

FIG. 27.   FIG. 28.

3. Stitch the tape on the *right* side while holding *the edge of the hem to the worker*. Be careful to slip the needle between the folds to commence, and to begin and end exactly at the extreme edges of the tape. Do not break the cotton, but pass the needle to the wrong side.

4. Fold the tape back over the stitches just made, and fell as far as the second crease (or to form the second side of a square), without taking the stitches through, or else *all* through. (*See* Fig. 28.) Pass the needle to the right side.

5. Stitch across to match the first row, and again bring the needle to the wrong side.

6. Fell the fourth side of the tape and slip the needle between the folds to finish. Hem the end. Figs. 29 and 30

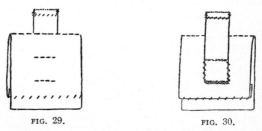

FIG. 29.   FIG. 30.

show the finished appearance (in miniature) on both right and wrong sides.

A Loop for a Towel.—The loop may be secured either to the

middle of one end of a towel or at one corner. The former plan
is the more simple arrangement for young pupils.

Each child should be provided with a small piece of calico,
about 4 in. by 3 in. (*i.e.*, 4 in. selvedge way by 3 in. weft way),
to represent the towel, and a piece of tape 6 in. long and about
half an inch wide.

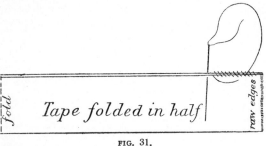

FIG. 31.

Directions for Working—

1 Fix a hem across the *weft* way of the piece of calico
illustrating the towel.
Make one-sixth inch
turn for the first fold,
and half an inch for
the second. This need
only be tacked, but
the diagram shows
the hem complete.

2. Mark the half of this
miniature towel by
creasing it in half
selvedge way, as it
would be folded to
hang on a towel-horse.

3. Double the tape to
mark the half as
shown in Fig. 31, and
sew the selvedges of
the tape together for
nearly an inch (more
than ¾ in.), begin-
ning at the raw edges.
Fasten off the sewing
very securely, and
flatten out the join
with the thumb nail.

4. Turn under the raw
edges of the tape for
¼ in. The sewing may

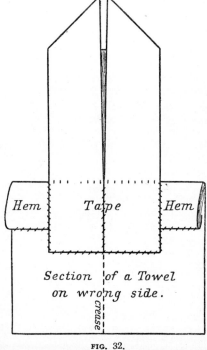

FIG. 32.

38

be on the outside, or inside, as preferred—it is on the *outside* in the diagram.

5. Place the line of sewing to the crease which marks the half of the towel, so that the *end* of the sewing comes *just to the edge of the towel.* (Fig. 32.)

The lower part of the tape *must be parallel* with the edge of the hem. Pin the tape in position and tack it.

6. Fell round the three sides of the tape, beginning at the right-hand side, and keeping the corners quite to a right angle —when felling over the thicknesses of the hem, *every* stitch should be taken well through, or else not any (the diagram illustrates the latter). Do not break the cotton.

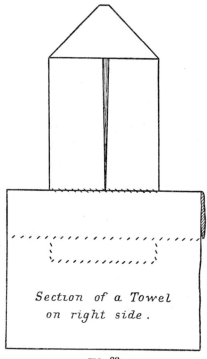

Section of a Towel
on right side.

FIG. 33.

7. Turn the work to the right side. Bend down the tape and with the same cotton sew the extreme edge of the fold of the hem to the folded tape. Finish off by slipping the needle between the thicknesses of the material. Fig. 33 shows the appearance when complete.

NOTE.—If preferred, the tape may be sewn to the edge first

and the felling worked afterwards. Instead of sewing the tape
to the hem, it may be kept flattened out and *stitched* on the
right side close to the edge.

To Attach a Tape Loop to the Corner.—Prepare the tape
exactly as shown in Fig. 31. Make a diagonal crease from the
corner of the towel, and place the sewing to the crease. Fell
the tape on the wrong side, and sew or stitch it on the right.
(Fig. 34.)

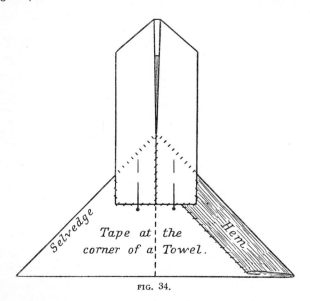

FIG. 34.

CHAPTER VII

HERRING-BONING

I. Introduction.—This stitch is used in making up flannel garments, or upon any woollen or thick material. Herring-boning is necessary to protect the raw edge, and so takes the place of a hem or fell and prevents ravelling. It may be taught upon coarse flannel, and cotton about the thickness of the threads of material should be used for working. Coloured cotton is preferable.

The use of canvas for teaching purposes is now discarded, and the stitch practised, in the first instance, on a fold of flannel.

II. Description of the Stitch.—It is begun at the left-hand side, and is formed from left to right. It should be four threads deep, although threads should *not* be counted after the first few stitches are spaced. If these are not correct in shape the whole line is generally thrown out.

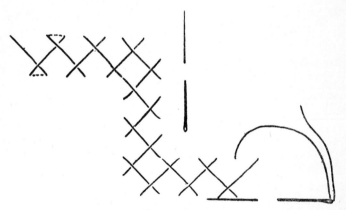

FIG. 35.—HERRING-BONING.

In Fig. 35 the relation of the parts of herring-boning is illustrated—the stitch at the top being opposite the space at the bottom and *vice versa*, while the *depth* of the stitch is equal to a stitch and a space together. The needle is always inserted horizontally.

It is as well to teach the turning of corners early, as this will be paving the way for the corners of a flannel patch.

Inner Corner.—Stop at the *upper* part of the stitch—insert the needle at the *lower* part as for another stitch, but point it perpendicularly as shown in Fig. 35—turn the work round

40

to the left hand and draw the cotton through—the inner corner will be formed if the needle is brought *out* to touch the *lower* part of the last stitch.

Outer Corner.—This is worked *exactly* the same as the inner corner, only changing the word *upper* to *lower*, and *vice versâ*, and *inner* to *outer*.

III. Preparation of Material.—For practice purposes, it is better to use flannel torn selvedge way, although in garments weft way of material has often to be worked. It is an open question as to which is preferable—*tearing* or *cutting* flannel. Many are in favour of the former, and *cutting the fringe off before herring-boning*. If flannel be torn selvedge way, this fringe is short, but weft way longer and more irregular in length. The woolly or fluffy side of flannel is the right. The threads can be seen more distinctly on the wrong side. The fluff is called the " nap," or " ply." In cloth, velvet, and plush, it takes the name of " pile." Garments should be always made up with the ply running downwards. The way of the nap is easily detected if the hand be brushed down the flannel. If little lumps of fluff are seen, the hand is rubbing against the nap.

When the fold has been turned the required depth, firmly fixed, and the frayings cut off, the work is ready for herring-boning. The tacking stitches must be put six threads from the raw edge, so that they are not in the way of the herring-boning.

An *even, square-threaded* flannel should always be selected for teaching purposes, and for this purpose Yorkshire flannel (cream-coloured) is the best, as it shows little difference between the right and wrong sides. No. 40 sewing cotton is the most suitable, certainly not finer than 50.

IV. The Stitch on Flannel.—*To Commence.* Hold the *raw* edge of the fold *towards* the worker. Slip the needle between the double material, and bring out four threads up on the fold ; make one or two backstitches to secure the cotton (Fig. 36), and work as described in Section II. The stitches should be made so that the *lower portion of the stitch comes exactly under the raw edge of the flannel*, and the little crosses of the *upper* row just opposite the spaces between the crosses at the *lower* row. (This should be specially noted, as there is a tendency to put the *lower* part of the stitch too near the last one, and so produce a slanting stitch.) All stitches should show through clearly, so that the reverse side looks like *two lines of running stitches*. Threads should not be counted after a few stitches are worked, but even distances gauged by the eye, leaving as much *between* each stitch as is taken *on* the needle. Sometimes that part of the stitch which comes on the fold is not taken through the two thicknesses of material. This is not suitable for practical purposes, as the stitch is not sufficiently secure for washing well.

To Join—Complete the *lower* part of the stitch—insert the needle as for an upper stitch, but slip it to the *left*-hand side of the *last* cross, making a backstitch on this stitch and slipping the needle along the fold—*cut* the cotton. (Fig. 37.) Commence with the new thread by slipping the needle some distance from the right and bringing it out two threads in front of the

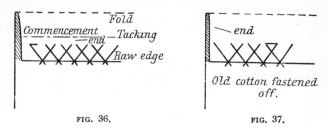

FIG. 36.   FIG. 37.

last half stitch (Fig. 38)—fasten with a backstitch. Fig. 39 shows the join complete with the two backstitches side by side.

On no account must *a knot* be used for commencement or joining.

To Fasten Off.—Always stop at the upper part of the stitch and put in the needle as if to make another stitch, but slip it between the fold to the left-hand side of the last cross as described for fastening off the old cotton before joining with new cotton. (Fig. 39.)

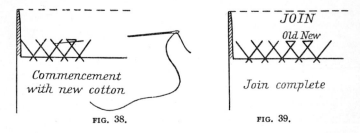

FIG. 38.   FIG. 39.

Herring-boning is worked upon the wrong side in garments, but in patching is shown on the right side as well.

V. Faults liable to occur are—

1. Commencement, joins, and fastening off insecure, inaccurately worked, and untidy.

2. Incorrect shape to stitch, the crosses of upper row not being *exactly* opposite the space in lower row, and *vice versâ*. (This is a common fault with beginners, who generally produce a leaning stitch to the right, caused by not putting the needle in a sufficient distance to the right in the *lower* part of the stitch.) An illustration of the cause on a blackboard will soon correct an error in this respect. As much material should be taken *on* the needle as is left *between* each stitch.

The tendency is to leave *more* threads *between* the stitches than are taken on the needle.

3. The upper row of stitches not kept sufficiently high up on the fold, and the lower row not effectually covering the raw edge.

4. The top part of stitch not taken through the thicknesses of material.

5. Cotton pulled too tightly, and so producing a pucker.

VI. Remarks.—The most suitable apparatus to use in teaching herring-boning is plain house flannel and yarn or thick wool (in contrasting colours) which can be passed through the eye of a chenille or sail needle.

CHAPTER VIII

STITCHING

I. Introduction.—Stitching, or back-stitching as it is sometimes called, seems to have fallen into disuse upon hand-made garments, probably from the amount of time taken to produce a quantity of any length, and as this is the stitch which the sewing machine imitates so quickly and accurately.

It is advisable to dispense with stitching as much as possible on garments, as it is misapplying valuable time which may be more profitably spent on more important branches of needlework. Stitching is so exclusively a machine stitch that the minimum only should be done by hand.

Machine stitching well worked is ornamental and very effective, but few workers are able to produce *excellent* stitching by machine, as it requires much practice, a very careful adjustment of the tension, and far more skill in handling than many are inclined to allow.

In the outcry which has been made by some educationists against fine needlework, stitching has been very much condemned as being harmful to the eyesight. This is undoubtedly true if the stitch is worked in drawn threads on fine longcloth (a process which would never be required in household use), but if taught on a *coarse* loose-threaded calico no objection can possibly be made to any girl learning to stitch, and the knowledge will be invaluable for all kinds of practical needlework. The working is not in the least tedious if common sense is applied to the teaching.

II. Uses of Stitching.—(*a*) For ornamentation—when worked coarsely upon neckbands, wristbands, sleeves, fronts of garments, etc., to give a neat finish. (*b*) For strength—when used for setting on tapes and buttons, joining seams in bodices and skirts, and making neat the lower part of placket holes and openings, when one portion of a garment is wrapped over another, and for all purposes where security is important.

III. Preparation of Material.—Stitching is worked selvedge way when it is used upon bands for ornament, and for teaching purposes stitching should always be shown selvedge way, as the finished appearance is better.

It has been customary for many years to withdraw a thread from the material in order to assist the evenness in working the size of the stitch. This practice is now entirely given up,

44

and other means are generally preferred to secure regularity, such as a crease ; a line of tacking ; a mark scratched with the needle. Even distances should, as far as possible, be gauged by the eye, whether the stitch is used for ornament or for strengthening purposes.

Before stitching is taught practice should be given in preparing bands (*see* Chap. V).

For teaching purposes, a thin, loose, and coarse make of calico or linen should be chosen. Linen which is sold for drawn thread work is soft and not fine.

IV. Rule for the Stitch.—This can easily be taught on small strips of coarse double material, fine *embroidery* cotton being used for the thread. Stitching is worked from right to left.

To Commence. Bring the needle through between the folds at the right-hand end of the strip. Count, for example, two threads

FIG. 40.—STITCHING.

to the right from where the cotton comes out, insert the needle in a continuous line and bring it out the same number of threads in front of the cotton, making four threads on the needle in all. (Fig. 40.) Every stitch is formed in the same way, care being taken to put the needle back *exactly* at the end of the last stitch, which will avoid any threads being left between the stitches. Discontinue counting threads as soon as the size of the first stitch is decided upon.

Three (or four) threads may be taken up, making six in all, or even more, provided regularity is kept. The appearance of

I. Regular back   *II. Irregular back*

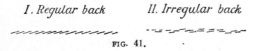

FIG. 41.

the wrong side is also a matter of some importance. At the back it will be seen that there is a long stitch, *i.e.*, double the length of the one in front. When the needle is inserted, it should be *below* this long stitch, so as to avoid splitting it. This necessitates giving the needle a little slant (slightly in the direction of the hemming stitch), and so produces a cable on the wrong side. This cord-like appearance is not difficult to obtain, if the first finger of the left hand just guides the stitch at the back, while the needle is put in, and the regularity of the right side is thereby increased. (Fig. 41.) This is a detail, but can hardly be looked upon as a grave fault, and should not be criticised with beginners, although for a high standard of efficiency it is sometimes regarded as essential. With children's work little need be said about the wrong side, provided the stitches are well taken through, as regularity can only be obtained at the cost of slow studied stitches, and this deprives needlework of its practical value.

V. Joins.—The needle should be passed to the wrong side as if another stitch were required, one stitch should be sewn over the stitches at the back, the needle slipped between the folds for at least half an inch, and the cotton cut off. The new cotton should be slipped along the folds *just* above or below the stitches on the right side, and brought out in the required position for the new stitch. The first few stitches will be worked over this end and make it quite secure.

A join or finishing-off should not be in the least conspicuous, as neatness is the chief feature.

VI. Faults likely to occur—

1. Material badly prepared (a most usual fault).

2. Commencement and joins insecure and untidy.

3. Cotton pulled too tightly, and so producing holes between each stitch.

4. Threads left between stitches (the common fault with beginners).

5. Stitches not uniform in size, and in an irregular line.

6. Uneven appearance on the wrong side, caused by putting in the needle sometimes above the backstitch and sometimes below it (hardly to be considered as a fault).

7. Split stitches, resulting from taking only the upper fold instead of making the needle pierce the double material.

CHAPTER IX

SEAMS IN FLANNEL

I. Introduction.—There are several methods of joining together two pieces of material in which the texture is of such a nature that the seam would be clumsy if joined by sewing and felling.

Flannel, flannelette, cloth, serge, or any similar material, may be worked in the method described.

Seams are usually made selvedge way or on the selvedge slant.

METHOD I

This plan is suitable for any undergarment.

Place the two right sides together, keeping the back edge about a quarter of an inch above the front, and tack securely rather less than half an inch *below the back edge*. Join the material just above the tacking by run stitching, (*i.e.*, a backstitch, and a few stitches of running, Fig. 42). In making the backstitch, the needle should be brought *out in the same place* that the cotton comes from, and then the running stitches taken on the needle; the stitches will then appear regular on the reverse side. Three-eighths of an inch is a suitable depth for the running, but this is sometimes modified by the quality of the material—in a very fine flannel the seam might with advantage be rather less than three-eighths of an inch, and similarly in a coarse-threaded material it might be advisable slightly to increase the depth.

Cut off any fraying from the back edge, and open the material so that the hand can be placed along the right side.

There is a tendency to pucker the seam on the right side when fixing down the fell for herring-boning (it is most essential that it is fixed). The fell should be almost " strained " in the fixing, and a good plan when handling a fell of this kind is to hold the straight edge *away from the worker*, and put in the tacking while the work is in this position, which will entirely prevent puckering. The tacking thread should be about six threads *below* the raw edge.

The work must then be turned round, and the herring-boning worked with the raw edge towards the worker. (Fig. 43.)

The above method is adopted for gored seams.

The front breadth of a garment is usually gored on both sides, but the side portions are often slanted only on one side, so that the opposite edge remains on the *straight*. In making skirts of any description, it is customary to join a *gored* edge to a *straight* edge, and this requires more skilful handling than joining material in which *both* edges are straight. (Exceptions to this rule are often made in Dressmaking, but do not call for comment in the making of underclothing.)

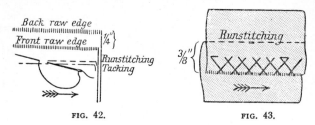

FIG. 42.   FIG. 43.

Fig. 44 shows the position of placing the two edges, with the *right* sides facing. In fixing the seam the slanting side must be *eased*, or held lightly against the straight side, not in any way to pucker the work, but just to keep it *perfectly flat*, remembering that the gored side has a tendency to stretch. A strong rule exists that any edge likely to give or become full should be held *towards* the worker, so that the left thumb may assist in the guiding. The left thumb acts the same part in the human machine—the hand—as a presser foot would do in a sewing machine.

The seam is worked exactly as described above.

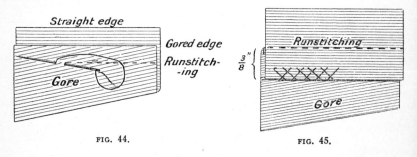

FIG. 44.   FIG. 45.

Fig. 45 shows the straight edge herring-boned over the gored, but the tacking thread is not shown.

Sometimes the entire process is reversed.

METHOD II

This makes a flatter seam than the former, but is not so strong, and would be unsuitable where the seam has to bear any strain in wearing. The method is most suited to baby clothing on account of its flatness.

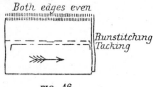

FIG. 46.

The two edges would be placed *evenly*—fixed—and the run-stitching worked at *barely* ⅜ in. (less if the flannel is thin) below the raw edges. (Fig. 46.) The seam is then flattened out right and left, and the edges herring-boned as shown in Fig. 47.

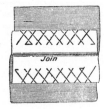 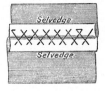

FIG. 47.   FIG. 48.

METHOD III

The preparation of this arrangement is similar to the previous method, but after the work is flattened out the herring-boning is worked *over* the join, which would leave the edges raw, and is rarely applied in garment making, and should be criticised as an untidy seam. The method is sometimes used on flannelette, where the selvedges, being of a cotton nature and quite different from those of flannel, need not be removed. The edges are run-stitched (or machined) in the usual way, and the herring-boning being worked over the join on the wrong side helps to flatten the seam; still, everything considered, a run or sew and fell seam would even then be preferable.

Fig. 48 shows the appearance of the seam when complete.

Points for Criticism—

    1. Seam badly fixed—needlessly wide or too narrow.

    2. Seam puckered on the right side.

    3. Insecure run-stitching and herring-boning faulty. (*See* Chap. VII.)

CHAPTER X

PLEATING

I. Definition and Use.—A pleat is a fold of material of any width secured in place and kept firm by a band which is felled across the pleats.

Pleating is not suitable for garments which need ironing, as the material cannot so easily be flattened; but, by its adoption, a greater variety of garments can be made by young pupils, as well-formed pleats are infinitely to be preferred to clumsy gathering and setting-in.

Pleating is the usual method of arranging the fullness of flannel into a band.

Children should be quite familiar with the preparation of a band (Chap. V) before pleating is taught.

Lined or extension paper is most helpful in teaching pleating, as the perpendicular red lines secure a uniformity in the folding; striped flannelette is also an excellent material for the purpose. It is advisable in the early stages to teach the formation of pleats without any attention to a band.

II. Preparation of Material.—Pleating is made on the right side and is usually formed the weft way, so that the folds are made *with the selvedge*.

Pleats vary in size from about $\frac{1}{4}$ in. to 1 in., according to the garment for which they are required.

A pleat needs three times its width to form it, *e.g.*—

1. The upper part of the pleat.
2. The under part.
3. The space for the pleat to rest upon.

Pleats may be formed in two ways—

(*a*) Each pleat may *just touch* its neighbour; or,

(*b*) A space of *single* material may be left between one pleat and the next.

In the first instance, 3 times the length of material according to the length of band is necessary; and in (*b*) $2\frac{1}{2}$ times the length must be allowed, supposing the space between each pleat is equal to *half* its width. Sometimes more space is necessary, when $2\frac{1}{4}$ times would suffice.

Arrangement of Pleats.—The centre front or back of a garment should be marked, and the pleats must either face *towards or* *from* this centre. In aprons, the pleats usually turn *from the front* and face towards the back.

It is very essential that the corresponding pleat on either side of the centre should match in point of size.

It is sometimes preferred that the pleats face all one way.

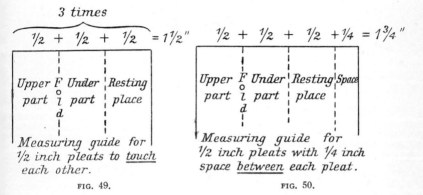

3 times

½ + ½ + ½ = 1½"   ½ + ½ + ½ + ¼ = 1¾"

Upper part	F o l d	Under part	Resting place

Measuring guide for ½ inch pleats to *touch* each other.

FIG. 49.

Upper part	F o l d	Under part	Resting place	Space

Measuring guide for ½ inch pleats with ¼ inch space *between* each pleat.

FIG. 50.

III. Directions for Fixing—

1. *For Pleats to touch each other.* Take a paper measure 3 times the width of the pleat required and crease it into 3 parts. The illustration shows a measuring guide for ½ in. pleats intended just to meet on the upper and under side. (Fig. 49.)

2. *For Pleats with a space between each other.* To the above guide, add the space required, which in Fig. 50 is equal to *half* the width of the pleat.

Measure along the top raw edge of the material with the guide, crease the fold, and secure it with a *small* pin. Place the measuring guide at the *edge* of the thickness of the pleat (as felt on the under side) and repeat the folding.

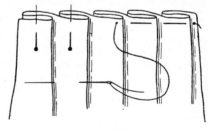

FIG. 51.

When all the pleats are arranged, tack them in position close to the edge.

Fig. 51 shows pleats touching each other and facing one way.

Fig. 52 shows pleats with a space between each other, and facing right and left of a centre crease. The marks XX indicate the plain material on either side of the middle. The folding should commence from X.

To arrange Pleats into a Band. Prepare the band and tack it as described on page 56, Heading VIII. Mark the half and quarters of the band and material, and pin the band to these divisions to determine the space for the pleating. In garments it often happens that the excess of material is only twice the

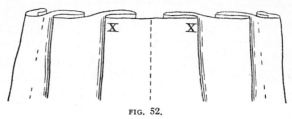

FIG. 52.

length of the band, in which case the entire width of the pleat must be left between for space.

The band must be fixed on the right side at *an even distance* (*about ¼ in.*) from the edge of the pleats. The band should be *stretched* across the pleats and held quite tightly in fixing.

The band is felled on the right side and the continuous cotton used to sew up the corner. The back of the band is then fixed *just to* (not *on*) the felling line, and worked exactly as for the right side, the remaining corner being sewn up with the same cotton.

Fig. 53 shows a completed specimen.

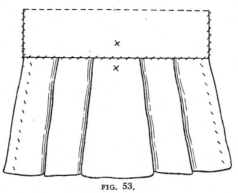

FIG. 53.

IV. Points for Criticism—

1. Material badly prepared.

2. Pleats irregular and unsuitable in size to the garment in making, and setting clumsily.

3. Puckered appearance of band, and turnings too deep under the band.

CHAPTER XI

GATHERING—STROKING—SETTING INTO A BAND

GATHERING.

I. Definition.—The word " gather " means to collect or draw together into a mass, and is the process used when a full part of a garment is required to be set into a shorter and narrower portion of material, called a band.

II. Reasons for Usage.—(1) Certain parts of garments need to be loose fitting, in order to give freedom and gracefulness to the body and play to the limbs ; and to ensure tidiness, comfort, and regularity, this fullness is gathered and distributed equally along a band, *e.g.*—

1. Skirts are gathered into waistbands.
2. Sleeves are gathered into wristbands.
3. Upper parts of garments are gathered into neckbands.

(2) Garments which are gathered present a much nicer appearance when ironed than if pleating had been used, because the point of the iron can be taken close to the band, and so all the surrounding material can be flattened out and smoothed.

III. Preparation of Material.—The gathering stitch is usually worked *weft* way, so that the selvedge runs *down the sides*. Gathers set so much better if worked the weft way of the material, and the stroking cannot be so well done unless this is attended to. In garments it is often necessary to gather on the *weft slant*. In order to ensure the gathers being arranged equally into the band, it is necessary to mark the half and quarters of the material to be gathered. These distances are best marked with cotton, about 1 in. below where the gathering is to be done.

The gathering stitch should be worked upon the *right* side of the material, about ¼ in. or a trifle more from the edge. The stitches run parallel with the weft threads, or from selvedge to selvedge. It is a help towards keeping the stitch straight, if a crease be made by flattening down the wrong side over the right, and turning it up again. The gathering cotton can then be kept along this crease—upon no account must a thread be drawn.

It is advisable to use coarser cotton than that in ordinary use upon the garment. If working with No. 60, for gathering No. 40 would be suitable, *and the end should be threaded as it comes from the reel.* Many people gather with double thread, so that if one thread should break, the other may be likely to hold. It is not advisable to *teach* the stitch with double cotton, as it is liable to get knotted, but it may be used at the discretion of

53

the worker, on thin material for example, where a coarse needle would perhaps leave marks in the fabric.

IV. Rule for the Stitch.—Never use a knot to secure the end of cotton ; take up a few threads in the crease ; leave ½ in. of cotton, which should be held down with the second finger ; take the same amount of material on the needle again, and draw through till a small loop remains ; catch in (with the needle) the little end of cotton left ; tighten ; take another backstitch, and pull *well* to test if the cotton is secure.

FIG. 54.—GATHERING STITCH.

Another method of fastening on is as follows : Make a slip loop by holding the extreme end of cotton over the first finger-tip of the left hand, bringing the cotton round the finger and holding it under the left thumb ; insert the needle through the loop of cotton which is over the nail and draw the long end through with the needle, which will make a small slip knot ; withdraw the needle and take up a few threads in the creased line for gathering ; pull the cotton through till it is near the slip loop, and then catch the needle into the loop and draw tightly.   This is a very secure fastening.

The quantity of material taken on the needle should be *exactly half* of that passed over.   Take up 2 threads and miss 4, or, if fine material, 3 and 6 or 4 and 8.   If this regularity be not kept, the whole effect is spoiled.   Threads should not be counted after the first few stitches, but the proportion kept by the eye.

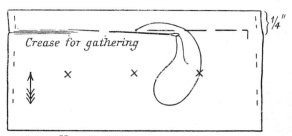

FIG. 55.—GATHERING-IN PROCESS OF WORKING.

The diagram shows the material on the flat as the gathering thread is put in.   This is advisable when teaching, because any irregularity is easily detected if the work be kept flat, and in the making of garments which have to be folded from time to time, it is better that the material should not be drawn together until ready for stroking, as the garment will be less likely to become creased.

If a long piece has to be gathered, new cotton must be taken at the half and quarters and the old thread left hanging.   When proficiency is attained, several stitches may be taken on the needle before drawing the cotton through, and the left thumb can then push the material on to the needle, which is the plan adopted by all expert workers. The stitch is usually worked upon *single* material, but in gathering for the waist of a frock or petticoat it would often be upon *double* stuff. Fig. 55 shows the work in progress.

STROKING.

V. Preparation.—When the gathering is complete, the cotton should be drawn up moderately tight, and a pin, taking up a *few threads*, placed *exactly* by the end of cotton, which should be secured round the pin three or four times. (Always put pins in work for this process with points upward.) It is a help to successful stroking if the gathers are pulled above and below the gathering thread, and so partly straightened into place.

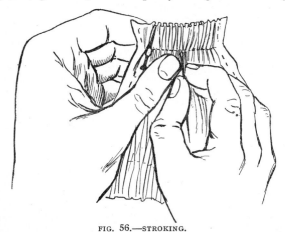

FIG. 56.—STROKING.

The aim in stroking is to place the gathers evenly side by side in little rucks, ready for setting-in. This evenness disappears the first time a garment is washed, the only result being the regularity of the gathers in the band. The stroking might be done with the right-hand thumb and forefinger, if the gathers are sufficiently large to allow it. The eye of a fine sewing needle or darning needle, or the point of a rug or carpet needle may be used—*not* the point of a pin.

VI. The Act of Stroking.—This is done upon the right side, and begins at the left hand. Hold the material between the left thumb and forefinger so that a few gathers are at the top of the finger ; the thumb must be kept *below the gathering thread ;* hold the stroking needle between the tip of the right-hand thumb and forefinger ; it should point quite flatly or horizontally into the groove between the gathers just as the hands of a clock at noon. Each gather must be gently raised up with the needle, laid under the left thumb, and pressed firmly. The stroking needle need not guide the gather for more than $\frac{1}{2}$ *an inch* below the gathering thread. Great care is necessary to avoid " scratching " or " striking " the fabric, as it is so soon injured by careless stroking, and consequently splits in the washing. While the needle is arranging the gathers, there is no occasion to make any sound by its use. The gathering thread may require tightening as the stroking proceeds. When all the gathers are arranged *below* the thread, the work should be turned completely round, and the material stroked which will be covered by the band, or that which was *above* the gathering thread in the first process. This is very essential. Fig. 56 illustrates stroking in progress.

Another method of stroking is as follows : Instead of holding the gathers facing worker as directed above, place the material so that the gathering thread is almost at right angles with the worker, and the thumb half-way above and below gathering thread ; then, with the stroking needle, lay each gather alternately above the thread and below it, under the pressure of the left thumb.

SETTING GATHERS INTO A BAND.

VII. Proportion of Band to Material Gathered.—The *rule* is that the band should be *half* the length of the material required for gathering. An inch or two more of gathering material to every $\frac{1}{4}$ yd. of band greatly improves the fulness. It is often necessary, in making garments, to allow *less* material than stated above ; but, of course, the gathers are scanty and do not set so well.

VIII. Preparation of Band.—If a *straight* band is required, it should always be torn, so that *the length is selvedge way of the material*, because these threads are strong and firm, and the band will wear much better, besides presenting a nicer appearance. Shaped bands, such as are often used for yokes, require more skill in putting on. The width of the band is a matter of taste —it quite depends upon which part of the garment is in making.

A selvedge should not be used, as it often causes the band to pucker.

The detailed directions for preparing a band as given in Chapter V must be most carefully followed. The edges of the band must be straight and true to a thread, or the whole effect of the setting-in will be spoiled.

Tack up the sides, leaving a quarter of an inch free at the folded corners, as this will admit of the back part of band being kept up out of the way, while the gathers are set in on the right side. Halve and quarter the band to correspond with divisions of garment.

IX. Fixing the Band.—Remove the pin which has secured the gathering thread. Loosen the gathers to length of band. Have in readiness a few *small* pins (Lills). Place the front edge of the half of band on the half of the gathering material, *just to* *the cotton.* Secure by a pin placed thus : Pass the point of the pin through the band, through the gathers, and up through the band again. (Fig. 57 shows method of pinning.) This will hold firmly (children need to have this clearly demonstrated by the

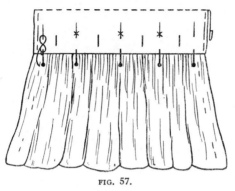

FIG. 57.

teacher). Treat the quarters in the same way, and the beginning and end. Draw up the gathering thread till it is just even with the edge of band, and secure the thread around the pin. If only a small quantity of gathers is to be set in, it is hardly necessary to tack the work, pinning being sufficient ; but, should tacking be needed, the following method is more suitable than ordinary tacking : Bring needle through on the right side of band about ¼ in. up from the edge which rests on the gathers ; put needle in exactly below where cotton came out, and take a slanting stitch about ⅛ in. from the first one, bringing needle out ¼ in. up on the band as before. This will produce a small *upright* stitch on the right side, and will admit of the gathers being shifted with the needle, so as to regulate them easily. (Fig. 57.)

X. Position of Work for Setting-in.—*Hold the band* towards the worker, not parallel with the body, but inclined to it at about an angle of 30°. Let the left-hand forefinger be placed just under a few gathers, and hold the band in place with the end of the left thumb. The right elbow must be kept well up from the side.

FIG. 58.—SETTING-IN STITCH.

XI. The Setting-in Stitch.—(Fig. 58.) Commence as for hemming by tucking the end of the cotton under the band and work a few hemming stitches across the hem. (1) Take up the ruck which forms the gather on a line with the gathering thread, and (2) turn the needle round so that the eye is turned away from the band, and the point is in readiness just to take the *extreme* edge of the fold of the band. In making the next stitch the needle should be put in exactly below (or as the work is being held, it is above) the place where the cotton came out for the previous stitch, *and behind the gather or ruck*. The little *upright* stitch (not quite so, if the gathers are scanty) will then fall *in the groove* formed by the gathers. The cotton must not be pulled in the least degree tightly, or puckering of the band is certain. The setting-in stitch is similar to the letter N, the straight part forming the right side. Fig. 59 shows the work in progress.

The gathers will need regulating with the needle as the work proceeds. Remove the pins as soon as convenient. When the

FIG. 59.—SHOWING THE POSITION OF THE NEEDLE IN SETTING-IN GATHERS.

end of the band is reached, the corner may be sewn up with the same cotton as is used for the setting-in without breaking off, and the folded corners of the band pressed very tightly between the thumb and finger. When the side is sewn, slip the needle between the fold of the band and cut the cotton.

XII. Wrong Side of the Band.—Before fixing this, thread the needle with the gathering thread, and fasten it off on the wrong side. The wrong side of the band will need careful fixing, and the selvedge fold should be stretched as much as possible. Keep the edge *well up* from the line of the gathering, *just a trifle* above it is perhaps preferable (the working will bring it into place), as the whole appearance is so easily spoiled by a careless treatment of the back of the band. Set-in the *wrong* side in just the same way *as the right*. It will be much easier, as the gathers are all arranged. Be very careful that no stitch shows through on the right side. Do not pull the cotton too tightly, or it may cause the band to pucker on the right side. Sew up the corner with the *same* cotton and fasten off as before.

XIII. Faults met with are—

1. Gathering material wrongly prepared, so that the stitches are worked with the selvedge instead of the weft way.

2. Irregular gathering—line of stitches not at a suitable distance from the edge. Knots for commencement.

3. Faulty stroking. (1) Material harshly scratched, so that a line of marks is left on the stuff ; or (2) insufficient stroking, so that gathers are not regularly placed for setting-in.

4. Band prepared the wrong way of the material—badly turned.

5. Gathers unevenly distributed along the band.

6. Band clumsily fixed on. Gathering thread showing.

7. Incorrect stitch in setting-in. Every gather should have *its own* stitch, which must be *behind* the gather and in the groove, not slanting across the gather as for hemming.

8. Band twisted, often caused by want of care when working the wrong side. Back setting-in stitches showing on right side.

9. Corners untidy, bulky, and insecure. Ends of cotton left.

10. General puckered appearance, and clumsy effect of the whole.

XIV. Remarks.—The regular appearance of the right side of the work is much improved by gently re-stroking the gathers after the setting-in is finished.

To teach gathering successfully to a class, it is imperative that the teacher should provide herself with a large specimen upon which to illustrate each step. A piece of coarse towelling and a coloured thread are a ready and an excellent means of demonstrating each stage of the work, and it is most essential that one step shall be mastered before proceeding to the next.

CHAPTER XII

BUTTON-HOLING AND BUTTON-HOLES

I. Introduction.—Probably no stitch in plain needlework needs such careful attention to detail as the above. The button-hole stitch should be taught to girls about ten or eleven years of age, and exactly the same principles should be adopted by any worker, the only difference being in the " style," which can only be acquired by practice. Skill with the fingers is most necessary to successful manual work of any kind, as the thumb and forefinger assist greatly in manipulation. Too much stress cannot be laid upon the *position* in which the work is held. Teachers should impress upon pupils the necessity for grasping the material firmly between the thumb and finger. To acquire skill with this grip should be one of the aims of a needle-woman, as it is this feature which gives that neatness of execution which so stamps " well-finished work." Button-hole working affords excellent practice in precision, accuracy, deftness with fingers, and neatness, as it is an invaluable lesson in training both hand and eye.

II. Description.—A button-hole is a " slit," worked all round with a *knotted* edge. The ends of the slit can be varied by making them either square or barred, or round, according to that part of the garment for which the hole is needed.

III. Reasons for Usage.—In conjunction with a button, it is a means of fastening together two separate parts of any garment which need a close fit (not necessarily tight) to render the garment comfortable to the wearer and neat in appearance.

IV. Different Stages in which a Button-hole should be Taught—

I. The actual stitch upon material which has *coarse* even threads. No slit should be cut. Fine embroidery cotton is generally considered the best thread for use, which should be about as thick as the threads of the material.

II. The same process only on a folded edge of calico, such as a band.

III. Combining the two kinds of ends in making a button-hole—still without a hole—sometimes called a blind button-hole.

[NOTE.—Stage I is frequently omitted and Stage II used as a means of teaching ; but the *general principles* of button-holing and the formation of the ends are more readily mastered if taught as in Stages I and III.]

IV. Practice in cutting slits with button-hole scissors; also with ordinary scissors, and, if preferred, with a penknife.

V. Working the slit in calico, with explanation about commencement, turning round corner, a barred end, and finishing off.

VI. A join in working the slit.

VII. A slit on the cross and the method of stranding.

VIII. Cutting and working button-holes in thick material.

Each of the above steps will now be taken in detail.

Stage I.—Method of Making the Stitch on Coarse Material—

1. Hold the material the right side uppermost over the first and second fingers, keeping it in its place with the thumb and the third and fourth fingers.

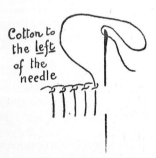

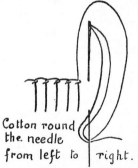

FIG. 60.—FIRST POSITION OF COTTON.

FIG. 61.—SECOND POSITION OF COTTON.

In plain needlework the button-hole stitch is generally worked from *left to right*.

2. Bring the needle through to the right side of the material about an inch from the left edge and an inch down (leave a finger length of cotton, which can be darned in neatly on wrong side when the stitches are all worked, or caught in with the needle as the work proceeds).

3. Put the cotton *up away from worker, towards the left hand.* Most people do this mechanically, but it is necessary to *enforce* this in teaching, otherwise one kind of wrong edge will be the result.

4. Insert the needle a little *to the right* on the material and take up about four threads perpendicularly. (Fig. 60.) The needle must always be put in to the *right* of the cotton.

5. While the needle remains placed thus, put the double cotton, that which comes from the eye of the needle, round the point from **left to right,** and draw upwards from the worker, inclining to the left, as the tendency is for the stitch to slant to the right. The cotton close to the loop may be caught up with the finger and thumb of the right hand in pulling the knot home. (Fig. 61.)

6. Each stitch is made in the same way, *one* thread being left between every time, as this allows room for the little knot which forms the edge and so keeps the stitch upright.

The position of the cotton with regard to the needle in Figs. 60 and 61 must be carefully noted—

1st Step. The cotton is away to the *left* of the needle.

2nd Step. The double cotton or that which comes from the eye of the needle is put round the point from *left to right.*

Any other position of the cotton will result in a wrongly formed edge.

There is a tendency for the cotton to drop to the *right* of the needle in the first step, and there is an inclination to put the cotton round from *right to left* in the second step, both of which errors are of very common occurrence, and each produces a different kind of edge to the stitch. It is advisable for experienced workers to be familiar with the incorrect edges, so that they may be detected at a glance.

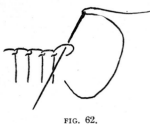

FIG. 62.

Another method of working the button-hole stitch is as follows : Adopt Nos. 1, 2, 3, and 4 as described above ; then draw cotton through till a small loop remains ; catch the needle in this loop from the back, *i.e.*, from the *under* part, and draw upwards. (Fig. 62.) Many people consider this the easier method. It is preferable to *teach* the former, and introduce the second way when proficiency is gained. The latter is decidedly a successful way of using up a small end of cotton, and perhaps is rather quicker when the eye is trained just to leave the loop a sufficient size; but with a child this seems the difficulty. Each teacher, however, must decide for herself which method she prefers and definitely teach it, not combining the two methods in a short space of time.

Stage II.—The Same Process as above on a Folded Edge.— The band on the gathering exercise affords a suitable place for practice in this stitch. The edge to be button-holed should be held firmly between the left thumb and forefinger, *the thumb nail being kept just below the place where the needle will be inserted.* The left forefinger should be slightly bent towards the chest, and the right arm must be kept well up from the side, as this enables more tension to be kept upon the thread. The end of the cotton can be slipped along the fold of the material, and brought out exactly at the edge; the stitches will be worked over the end of cotton, thus securing it. The aim at this stage should be to produce regular and even knots, as firm as a piece of wire, with the stitches all uniform in depth ($\frac{1}{8}$ or $\frac{1}{10}$ inch) and at right angles to the edge. The stitches must be worked *very quickly*.

Stage III.—Round End on Coarse Material.—This may be worked in three ways: (1) With a knotted edge as for ordinary button-holing; (2) with a twist of cotton at the edge, formed by putting the cotton from *right to left*—just the reverse position to the proper stitch; (3) simple over-casting, which is described below. The latter method is usually adopted. The round end is often called the "eyelet-hole end," as it is worked after the manner of an eyelet-hole. The round end of the

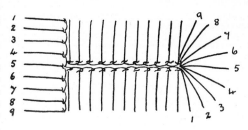

FIG. 63.—BUTTON-HOLE COMPLETE.

button-hole should *always* be placed to the end of the band, as it gives room for that part of the button which is taken up in the fastening. Fig. 63 shows the method of working. Completely finish the first side—the material must be gradually turned round as required. In detail, the corner may be described as follows: In order to work round to the other side, and form a semicircle, nine stitches are necessary (three on the slant, three on the straight, and three on the slant again), each of which is worked *into the same place*.

First stitch: Needle to be put in as though *another stitch* were needed for first side, but without making a knot, merely over-casting, or sewing backwards.

Second stitch: Insert into the same place, and bring the needle out a little to the right and a little farther round towards making a semicircle.

Third stitch: Same as the second.

Fourth, fifth, and sixth stitches: Insert into the same place; these three stitches are worked straight, one above each other; the fifth stitch should be on a line with the supposed slit.

Seventh, eighth, and ninth stitches: These stitches will correspond with the third, second, and first, and so complete the semicircle.

When the needle is inserted for the ninth stitch, the cotton should be *four* threads below the edge. This is clearly in the wrong place for working the second side of the button-hole ; *but put the cotton up away to left hand, and work as for the ordinary stitch with a knot at edge,* which will complete the ninth stitch of round end, and at the same time form the first stitch of second side. If the round end is worked with knots, not more than five stitches can be formed well, *e.g.,* two slanting, one straight, two slanting.

Square, Barred, or Braced End.—This end enables the hole to be kept partially closed when over the button ; it prevents the material from splitting, and gives a neat general finish ; nine stitches are usually worked. When the last stitch of the second side is completed, catch up the knot of the first stitch that was made (this will help to draw the slit together when a cut button-hole has to be worked), and bring the needle out in the *same place* as if making the last stitch of second side. To form the first stitch of the square end, put the needle into the *same space* as the thread comes from, and form the knots (which will be turned *towards* the hole) as for the *ordinary* stitch. The fifth stitch will be on a line with the supposed slit, and the ninth stitch will end where the first stitch of the first side began. Pass the needle to the wrong side, and run the cotton under the stitches at the back to finish off. Darn in the end left at the beginning similarly.

A teacher will have a difficulty, no doubt, in getting all her class to work a button-hole accurately, but even if a few members only work it perfectly, they will be the better for having mastered its details. It is well not to spend too much time upon the preliminary stages, but to proceed as soon as possible to the actual cut.

Stage IV.—Cutting the Slit in Calico.—It is very essential that the band be properly prepared, otherwise it is impossible to cut a good slit. Button-holes are always worked on two thicknesses of material, sometimes three. If a hole is needed on any part of a garment where there is only one thickness, a single piece of material must be felled on the wrong side for strength. Button-hole scissors should be used in preference to any others, but practice in the use of ordinary scissors is most necessary. *The diameter of the button must always regulate the length of the slit.* This length should be slightly (barely an eighth of an inch) longer than the width of the button, so that it does not require an effort to slip out the button. A good plan when cutting a hole in a garment is to place the button just where the hole is needed, and mark a scratch with needle, outside either side of button. A scratched line may guide the whole line of cutting, if preferred, as the material will be held quite flat. The distance the hole is cut from the edge of the band varies—usually it is from one-sixth to three-eighths of an inch—it must be quite free from the turnings of the band ; the hollow of the button-hole scissors will receive this piece of material while the slit is being cut.

Scissors with a screw for regulating the length of slit can be bought, but they are not recommended, as the screw soon becomes loose, and so its intended purpose fails. The *perfectly straight and clean cutting of the slit is indispensable*, as without this the whole effect is spoiled, no matter how well it may be worked. There are times (and these are very frequent) when it is necessary to cut a button-hole without button-hole scissors ; as these are so rarely found in the work-basket of the housewife, therefore it is well to know how to use ordinary scissors, which *must be small and the points sharp* (embroidery scissors are better than any others). *Large* scissors with *thick* blades are fatal to good cutting.

There are two recognised ways of cutting holes with ordinary scissors—

1. Stretch the band over the first and second fingers, and after the limits of the hole (according to the size of the button) have been pricked, *gently* scratch a line with the needle to guide the cutting—rest the needle against the inside part of the top of the right thumb and put the first and second fingers over the needle (first and third fingers if the thimble be on) —by this means it is easy to mark the calico quite straight by a thread for so short a length. Keep the band flat and insert the point of the scissors almost perpendicularly into one end of the slit in order to get a firm hold, and cut along by the guide line as far as the mark limits.

This method requires some practice, and the scissors *must* have good points ; but experienced workers invariably select this way of cutting, as it generally results in a *straight, clean* (not jagged) slit.

2. Another way of cutting is as follows : The material should be doubled exactly in half, and the needle passed through the two pin marks in order to keep the material quite straight, so that the folded edge is where the *middle* of the hole will come. A small snip should then be made with the scissors, and the material laid out flat again. Just the points of the scissors should be inserted in the small cut, and the slit extended to its required length by cutting a little at each end of it. Care is needed in cutting in this way, as in cutting through the fold, even if only a small snip be made, there is a danger of the under material slipping out of place. This method must be used if the scissors are not sharp at the points.

Children should be well practised, as button-hole scissors are not to be found in every household, and it is well to school every one to use the tools they will be likely to meet with. If a pen-knife be used, it must be very sharp, and the material laid flat on common wood, or a good-sized clean coin will answer the purpose, and the direction of the slit marked and cleanly cut. Practice should be given in cutting slits, selvedge way—weft way—on the cross—and also on material representing the front of a shirt or nightgown, as this is more difficult than a band, button-hole scissors being of no use. If the cutting of a button-hole is left to the choice of the worker, it should always be cut the selvedge way of material as for a band. The slit is easier to work, and presents a better appearance when done, if it is cut with the warp.

Stage V.—Method of Working in Calico.—The cotton used should be about as stout as the threads of the material, and slightly coarser than that in ordinary use on the garment, and sufficient taken to work the entire hole. For ordinary practice, No. 50 cotton is suitable, No. 40 for coarse material, while No. 60 is reserved for cambric. The end *must be threaded as it comes from the reel*, and not as broken from the bulk of the cotton, otherwise the fibres are rubbed the wrong way and knots are certain.

The length of cotton required should be ascertained before starting the working. As a rule, the length of cotton *in proportion of a yard* should equal the length of the slit *in proportion of an inch*, e.g., a slit of ¾ in. will need a thread of ¾ yd. in length. If the cotton is too long it is apt to tangle, and if too short a join is necessary, which should be avoided if possible on garments, although very essential for practice.

The work is held with the slit parallel to the worker, and *along* the finger, so that the slit is not stretched in the slightest degree.

The left thumb *nail* (which acts as a presser-foot would in a sewing machine) must be pressed *very* tightly on the material *just below* where the needle is inserted, so that *the point can rest on the nail* (the needle must not wobble about while the cotton is put round it, or uneven stitches will be the result).

The round end of the button-hole (*i.e.*, the part towards the *end* of the band), must be kept to the *right hand* of the worker. Hold the button-hole so that the stitch can be started at the *opposite* end to that where the round corner will come, or at that part of the slit which is *nearer the middle of the band, and what apparently is the most awkward place to handle.*

Commencement.—A good plan is shown in Fig. 64, where the needle is inserted between the fold quite half an inch above the left-hand side of the slit, and brought out *one* thread to the left of the slit. The first stitch formed is then a complete one. Sometimes a small backstitch is worked just to the left to secure the cotton in starting. The little end as shown can be held down with the third finger of the left hand, and can be cut off when the button-hole is finished. The needle may also be inserted upwards.

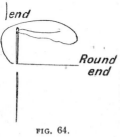

FIG. 64.

Continue working the side, being most careful to keep the back edge (the one against the forefinger) pressed well up so that it is caught in at every stitch. The back edge should be kept *a shade* above the front, so that the needle may be certain of piercing both thicknesses. The space between each stitch should be *the thickness* of the cotton.

As a rule, the quicker the stitches are made, providing they are accurate, the more regular and even the effect. The cotton should be drawn up with a *firm tension,* so that the edge is like a fine piece of wire. *In working the round end, pull the cotton* **very tightly,** *as it is not unusual to see an otherwise good button-hole with these stitches so loose that they may be lifted up with the needle.*

In calico work, the actual number of stitches which make up the round end may be disregarded, providing the end is worked *very* closely and tightly.

Before working the square end it is well to straighten the slit by pulling it in the direction of the hole. This will help to remove any puckering. Sometimes there is a difficulty in getting the regulation number of stitches in the square end, but *never* take the knots beyond the *first* and *last* stitches of the sides if even nine cannot be worked.

It is often impossible to get in nine stitches, as the threads of the material may not be the same thickness in both warp and weft. It is very necessary that the stitches of this barred or braced end be taken *through* the material. Some advise putting a few strands of cotton across the barred end, and then working the stitches *through the stuff* (not round the cotton alone). This is optional.

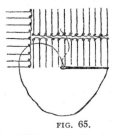

FIG. 65.

Fastening Off.—Pass the needle to the wrong side just where the last stitch ends, and secure the cotton by a backstitch before slipping the needle between the folds.

If a button-hole (cut well) has been worked badly, it is possible by using very sharp-pointed scissors to cut away the threads and re-work it, so that it may still be a good hole.

Button-hole with both Ends Square.—It is usual to make both ends of a button-hole alike if both ends will be exposed in wearing, as in the front of a nightgown.

The first side should be completed—the material turned entirely round and the second side worked—and the barred end is finished as though the slit were complete ; but, instead of fastening off, slip the needle to the *bottom of the last stitch of the first side* and work the second square end. (Fig. 65.)

Stage VI.—A Join in Working the Slit.—This is a very practical step and most essential, but one often forgotten in teaching. The join may be required from one or two causes—

(1) The snapping of the cotton.

(2) The length of cotton being too short to complete the slit.

If the thread should snap closely, one stitch should be unpicked so that an end of about ⅙ in. remains, or else the cotton must be cut to this length. (Fig. 66.) The needle should be threaded with

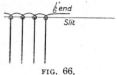

FIG. 66.

the new cotton and slipped upwards as shown in Fig. 67, bringing it out at the top of the knot of the last stitch. It is most necessary that the worked slit and the new cotton be held very firmly between the left-hand thumb and fore-finger during the commencement. The short end is then flattened towards the right and kept at the top of the raw edges. The stitches are then resumed in the usual way, care being taken to put in the needle at the back of the short thread, as shown in Fig. 68. This method of joining, if skilfully worked, can be made to appear almost invisible.

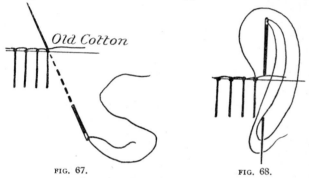

FIG. 67.   FIG. 68.

Stage VII.—Cutting and Working a Slit on the Cross. (Stranding.)

—Button-holes cut with the threads of the material present few difficulties when the principles of the stitch are mastered, because the cut edge does not (as a rule) show a tendency to fray in materials of a cotton nature ; but if the slit is required in any other position than that which is exactly by a thread, the difficulty in working is increased fourfold.

On yokes (for overalls, pinafores, or nightgowns, if the yokes are in *one* piece) or on shaped bands (if the material is arranged so that the threads are straight from the waist down to the hip) the button-hole has to be cut *across* the threads, and consequently stretches out of place with the least touch.

The position of the slit is best if defined with a crease, and the smallest, sharpest scissors that it is possible to procure should be used for the cutting. In order to prevent the slit from fraying and to give a firmness, strands of cotton should be put round it, and for this purpose about 4 in. of cotton in excess of that required for working the slit are necessary. The slit should be held so that the stranding can be commenced at that part of the slit which is *farthest away from where the round end is needed.*

Four little needle pricks should be made at the *ends* of the upper and lower part of the slit at not more than one-tenth of an inch below the cut edges (when experience is acquired these marks may be imagined, or more properly speaking, gauged with the eye).

Fig. 69 shows the commencement of the process of stranding. The needle is slipped between the folds of the calico, and brought out at A ($\frac{1}{10}$ in. below the slit). The needle is inserted at B and brought out at C, taking up the thickness of the material; in again at D and out at A, and so on, forming two sets of strands; while, when completing the second round, the needle is required to be brought out one thread to the left of the slit, as shown in Fig. 70. The stitches are then worked as usual, the needle being brought out *just below* the strands about $\frac{1}{8}$ in.

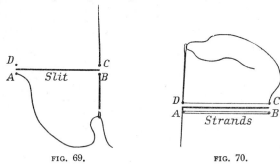

FIG. 69.   FIG. 70.

in depth, or the same distance below the slit as would be necessary if working on material where threads cannot be counted. Very great care is needed to prevent the strands getting to the top of the slit or rolling over to the wrong side. Plenty of left thumb-nail pressure is necessary to prevent this, and a very firm grasp of the cotton when pulling the knot home. The round end requires very close and tight working, and the square end must be kept a good shape and perfectly at right angles to the sides, there being a strong tendency to work this end very irregular in depth owing to the absence of the straight threads for a guide. Before working a barred or square end in a cross-way, button-hole strands are sometimes put across the material such as might be required for a hook, but the stitches must even then be taken quite through to the wrong side and *not* around the loose threads only.

Button-holes which are worked in woollen material, or in any material with a mixture of various kinds of threads, or even twilled calico, may have the button-holes stranded if preferred, although the slits may be selvedge or weft way. The utilitarian point of view must never be lost sight of in button-hole working, as the wearing consideration should occupy the first place; and if much strain is required at the round end (such as often happens at the waist of knickerbockers), it is advisable to work a close-knotted edge (the ordinary button-hole stitch) at the round end, otherwise it means repair after a very short time of wearing.

Stage VIII.—Cutting Holes on Thick Material.—If a button has a large shank, similar to those used upon cloth, it is necessary to actually cut away a piece of material in order to make the hole set well over the button. The best way of making this gap is as follows : Cut the slit in the ordinary way—then at the round end make a small snip at right angles to the slit—carefully slope away the superfluous material, which will leave a widened round end. Knots are worked all round the edge. (Fig. 71.)

FIG. 71.

V. Position of Holes in Garments with regard to Appearance and Utility—

1. **Shirts.**—Boys' and men's clothing always fastens *left* over *right*, probably from the old custom of carrying the pistol in the breast of the coat—hence the convenience of having garments so fastened. The button-hole at neck of shirt will be cut horizontally, those in the front perpendicularly, and on the *left* or *upper* side. These latter holes usually have braced ends. If studs are used, button-holes will be needed on the under or right side ; and in order to keep the stud securely fixed, it is necessary to cut the holes weft way, that is, at right angles to the button-holes on the upper side.

2. **Drawers and Petticoats.**—These garments fasten right over left or back over the front. The button-holes are cut selvedge way. Children's drawers, opening at the sides, and having a back and front band, usually have five button-holes ¾ of an inch in length—three on the front band and two on the back.

3. **Frock Bodices and Robes** fasten right over left, the hole being cut the weft way of stuff, *i.e.*, against the selvedges, (presuming that the material has been made up with the selvedge running from neck to waist). It is not unusual for the centre button-holes in a frock body to be cut parallel with the edge, but they will then have a tendency to gape open, unless the garment is loose-fitting.

Button-holes should be cut in material as follows—

Selvedge way—

(1) At the ends of all bands.
(2) In fronts of shirts and shirt-blouses.
(3) On yokes in overalls and frocks, if the selvedge is cut so that it is *across* the shoulders.

Weft way—

(1) In the fronts of dresses and blouses.

(2) The *middle* button-hole on the front band of children's knickerbockers.

(3) On the right hand or underside of linen-fronted (or dress) shirts.

(4) In the fronts of combinations.

Cross way—

(1) On a saddle yoke of overalls, frocks, or nightgowns.

(2) On a shaped band for a petticoat, but only if cut so that the selvedge runs *down* on the hips, which must necessarily bring the back of the garment on the cross ; and a join will be needed in front.

VI. Application of the Stitch for other purposes—

1. **Mending Kid Gloves.**—Work the ordinary button-hole stitch all round the raw edge of hole, then sew the knots of the stitch together on the right side. Use silk that matches the glove in colour, and the mend will be successful. This plan is very effectual when a glove tears at the gusset of the thumb, or a piece of kid may be put under the hole and the raw edge of glove button-holed to it. (A proper glove-needle, triangular in the shank, is recommended.)

2. **Tape Ends.**—If tape is narrow, the ends are often button-holed for neatness, as hemming would be clumsy.

3. **Openings in Garments.**—When one part of a garment is wrapped over the other, as in a placket-hole and the raw edges are seen on the wrong side, these may be neatened by button-holing.

VII. Summary for Button-hole Criticism—

1. A suitable position of the slit on the garment for which it is intended, so that the garment may wrap over sufficiently when fastened, or that it may not wrap too far beyond the amount allowed for the wrapping at the bottom of the placket.

2. That the slit is cut the correct way of the material according to the garment for which it is required.

3. A badly cut slit (not by a thread, if this direction is intended) or out of proportion to the button it is to carry. The slit must always pass easily over the button, so as not to occasion the least strain on the stitches of the slit.

4. Cotton (or other thread) unsuitable to the material on which the working is required, *e.g.*, button-holes on calico should not be worked with silk, which may be used for flannel garments if preferred. The cotton must be suitable in size to the threads of the material.

5. Faulty commencement caused by bringing the needle out *below* the slit instead of on a line with it.

6. Incorrect knot to the edge of the stitch formed by—
    (1) Allowing the cotton to drop to the *right* of the needle.
    (2) Putting the cotton round the needle from *right to left* when the direction of working is the reverse.

7. Stitches more or less than four threads (or a proportionate amount) in depth, and uneven as regards the thread on which they should be worked.

8. Stitches not pulled sufficiently tight or left too loose.

9. The cotton failing to bind in all the thicknesses of the material.

10. Looseness of round end is probably one of the worst faults.

    The relative position of the round and braced end misplaced as regards the end of the band, or different ends worked where both should be uniform, *e.g.*, where both are exposed.

11. Irregularity in the working of the ends respecting the number of stitches or the method of arranging them.

12. Insecure finishing off and ends of cotton hanging.

13. Generally poor work in style of execution through lack of finger skill and want of practice.

Note.—The more closely the attention is confined and the more rapid the working (consistent with accuracy), the greater the success of the button-hole, and this is the surest road to obtain that " knack " so essential to skilfulness.

Students are advised to practise " time tests " in this stitch. A good button-hole ($\frac{3}{4}$ in. in length) should be worked in seven or eight minutes.

CHAPTER XIII

BUTTONS

I. Remarks.—In fastening on a button, whether it may be linen, pearl, or metal of any kind, two essentials must be kept in view, whatever method of attachment is chosen, viz., *neatness* and *strength*.

A paper band, with a different coloured paper to represent buttons and suitable thread are excellent means of demonstrating this lesson.

Linen Buttons.—These can be bought in all sizes, known in the trade by "lines," *e.g.*, 10 lines, the smallest size made, and 36, the largest. Size 26 is about as large as a threepenny-piece. Buttons covered with 6-fold linen are the best quality. Buttons are usually attached to a card by a stitch of cotton, which is rarely in the centre ; and, although a mark is left by the attachment, it cannot be taken as a guide to secure uniformity of stitches in putting on the button. Linen buttons are put upon articles which are mangled, as the flat button passes through the pressing for some time without breaking. *Unpierced* buttons are recommended. Buttons should *always* be sewn on double material, *e.g.*, a hem, fold, or band. If it be necessary to attach a button to single stuff, fell a piece of material on wrong side to give strength, or the button will soon come away, bringing material with it.

II. Commencement.—The position of the button is found by lapping over the garment as required by the arrangement of the overwrapping of the placket or opening, passing the needle through at a short distance from *the end* of the button-hole which is to receive the button, *or the middle* if the slit is cut perpendicularly, and then carefully lifting the hole from the needle. Secure the cotton on the right side by a few back stitches, which will come under the button and be hidden. A knot is unnecessary and untidy.

III. Different Methods of Putting on a Button. (Fig. 72.)

1. **A Ring or Circle of Stitching.**—This is a very common method and has the advantage of being a very secure one, as it thoroughly tests the quality of the button. Various means are adopted to assist in making the circle—pricking a ring with a needle—faintly marking a circle with the round end of a pencil. The best plan is to press the round part of a key upon the linen. Buttons can be bought with a circular impression in the centre, but being rarely used in a

73

household, are not advisable for school use. The ring must not occupy more than *one-third* of the diameter of the button —slightly less is preferable. A child will need to be shown the way a button is " stabbed " for the purpose of stitching it ; also, when passing the needle from the wrong side of the material up through the button, just to let the point of the needle show, in order that it may be seen whether it is in the right place to make the stitches continuous.

2. **A Star,** of the same proportion as the ring of stitching, is suitable for small buttons. It consists of stitches radiating from the centre. To judge the number of stitches needed, it is well to bring the needle out at the centre, and make stitches representing N.S.E.W., and then subdivide these divisions according to the size of the button. By this method a star can be formed on the wrong side as well as right. This star may be stitched if thought desirable, or the threads may cross at the centre instead of piercing the button.

This method is only suitable for small buttons, and should not be used when strength is required.

3. **Two Parallel Rows of Stitching** *on a line with the button-hole slit* is a very secure way of attaching a button, and should be more often adopted than it is, especially in schools, as children find a difficulty in stitching a circle. The ends of the lines of stitching should not reach quite to the metal rim of the button. An oblong would be similar, and a guide line can be scratched on the button with the needle to help in keeping the stitches straight.

4. **Stitching in the Shape of an Ellipse** has much to recommend it.

5. **Two Loops** worked on the button, as for a hook, is a pretty and an ornamental way, but only suitable where very little strain is brought to bear upon the button, *e.g.,* pillow-cases, muslin frocks, fancy pinafores, etc.

6. **A Stitched Cross** is preferred by many.

7. **Small Upright Stitches on a Line with the Button-hole.** —This is similar to No. 3, only the stitches are perpendicularly side by side, instead of being in a line.

IV. Fastening Off.—Whichever of the above methods has been chosen—to finish, pass the needle *between* the button and the material, and wind the cotton round four or five times, to form a " shank." Be careful not to do this too tightly, so as to cause the material to be strained and dented on the wrong side, but with just sufficient tension to fulfil its purpose, viz., to keep from friction the stitches which have secured the button, and to make it set up from the band and so assist the buttoning and at the same time to strengthen.

This process of winding cotton to form a neck is called "stemming." When this is finished, pass the needle to the wrong side, make a backstitch, slip the needle between the fold, and cut the cotton.

Pearl Buttons.—These are pierced with four holes, through which the cotton is passed three or four times, to form either a square on the right side or a cross. The same plan would be adopted for commencement, stemming, and finishing off, as for a linen button. Articles for ironing only, such as muslin frocks, pinafores, and flannel shirts, have pearl buttons as a means of fastening, and these garments should not be mangled.

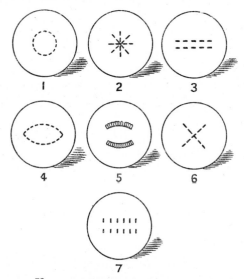

FIG. 72.—ILLUSTRATION OF THE ABOVE METHODS.

The dotted lines represent stitches of stitching, therefore in working, every stitch must touch the last, but it is hardly possible to show this in a drawing.

V. Criticism.—Whichever method of sewing on a button is adopted, it must be suitable to the garment, and the stitches strong and regular. They should not be too near the metal rim, so as to cause the button-hole to gape, nor too near the centre to render the sewing insecure. The wrong side of material must be neat and the fastening firm. The button should be stemmed, and the attaching stitches neither too tight nor too loose.

CHAPTER XIV

A RUN-AND-FELL SEAM

I. Remarks.—Running and felling is one method by which two pieces of material are joined together to form a seam. It is considered by some people a slovenly way of making a join, and named " scamp work " in consequence ; but, if well done, it is a quick and suitable way of joining material, especially if loose and thin in texture. It should not be taught until a sew-and-fell seam can be worked well.

The fixing and handling of a run-and-fell requires a skill which a young pupil does not possess, as if the seam is in the least puckered on the right side, the work is most unsightly. This kind of seam may be run and backstitched by a similar method to that used for making flannel seams (Chap. IX), and if the material is somewhat thick it should be worked in this way. Seams in flannelette garments should always be run and back-stitched, as running by itself is not sufficiently strong.

Seams which are very much curved under the arms (*e.g.*, the Magyar type) can be arranged to set flatly if the curve is *slightly* stretched *before* the material is fixed. On no account should a wide seam be worked in garments of this shape.

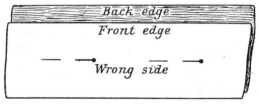

FIG. 73.

II. Directions for Fixing a Run-and-Fell.—Prepare the material so that the run-and-fell can be worked selvedge way or on the selvedge slant. Place the two pieces of material together with the right sides facing. Keep the back edge $\frac{1}{6}$ in. (narrower if fine material) above the front. Put in a few pins about $\frac{1}{2}$ in. down, to hold the material firmly. (Fig. 73.) Turn down the back edge *over* the front, and tack in place, being most careful to keep the edge straight. (Fig. 74.) The running stitches should come *just below the raw edge*, which will serve as a guide for keeping the stitches straight ; or a fold may be turned down and creased the required depth, then raised, and the stitches kept in the crease.

III. Rule for Running.—This is shown in Fig. 75, and is worked by taking up two threads on the needle and passing over two. On material this stitch is often modified by three and three, and unless the material be very thin, it is impossible to keep this proportion ; but in order to make the stitch appear regular on the reverse side, it is necessary to take up a little more material *upon* the needle than is passed *over*. If the material is of loose texture, two or three stitches may be taken

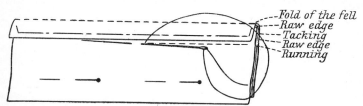

FIG. 74.—RUNNING IN PROGRESS.

on the needle at a time ; but if it is in the least harsh, running is almost a stitch by stitch process. *Every* stitch must show through clearly on the reverse side, or the work will be insecure if the stitches are split, and the space *between* each stitch must be *equal in size to the stitch itself* (there is a tendency to take a small stitch and leave a wide space).

Running should always be commenced with a backstitch.

Joins.—Fasten off the old cotton by making a backstitch, and then slipping the needle backwards above the running and between the folds of the material before cutting the cotton. Begin with the new cotton by slipping in the needle at some distance back from the fastening off, and bring it out so that *exactly the same pieces* of material may be taken up which will cover the old cotton for *at least half an inch*. The new cotton may be secured by a backstitch on any one of the running stitches, or in front of the old cotton. It is impossible for this join to come unfastened, and the work is strong and neat, the join consisting of thickened or double stitches.

FIG. 75.—RUNNING.

IV. Preparation for the Fell.—When the running is complete, do not remove the tackings which have secured the fold, as they will assist in keeping the fell even.

Open the double material so that the hand can be placed along the right side of garment, and tack down the fell perfectly flat and even, as upon this fixing will depend the " set " of the fell on the right side, which must not show the slightest fullness on the single material. It is in this particular that a run-and-fell presents a difficulty.

The fell must be " strained " in the fixing, and a good plan is to hold the *folded edge of the fell away from the worker* and put in the tacking thread while the work is in this position, which will entirely prevent puckering.

A skilled needlewoman would be able to dispense with the additional tacking of the fell, but for beginners it is essential.

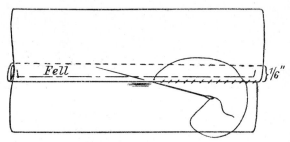

FIG. 76.—FELLING IN PROGRESS.

The fell is hemmed down in the ordinary way. (Fig. 76.) The material requires to be very skilfully handled, as the work is cumbersome and the stitches are liable to be badly shaped.

A portion of the fell should be gathered up in the left hand, as conveniently as is possible, and the hand and material moved as occasion arises.

The running and felling stitches should match in point of size.

V. Points for Criticism.—

1. Badly prepared fell, the depth being unsuitable to the garment—there is a tendency to make this kind of seam too wide.

2. Irregular, split, and poorly-shaped stitches in running and felling.

3. Fastenings insecure and untidy.

4. A puckered and clumsy appearance on the right side.

CHAPTER XV

A STRENGTHENING TAPE

I. Reason for Use.—A strengthening tape is placed on garments at the end of an opening or a seam, in order to give a neat finish, and to prevent the slit from tearing down in wearing—hence in many garments it is a substitute for a gusset. Tapes can be used at—

1. The under-arm of any pinafore, when the armhole is merely a slit (as in a cottage shape) or slanted to a point.

2. The side opening of children's drawers.

3. The lower part of placket-holes.

4. The end of a seam in a shirt sleeve, or the side seam—this is especially suitable for flannel, as a gusset is more clumsy.

5. Bags, in which a sew or run-and-fell seam has been used for joining material for a portion of the length, require narrow hems extending from the end of the opening; and the bottom of this opening is often strengthened with tape.

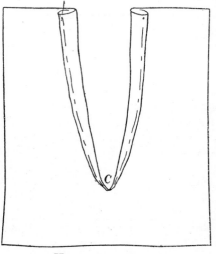

FIG. 77.—SHOWING HEMS TACKED.

II. Directions for Working.—The slit in the piece of material representing the garment should always be made the *selvedge* way of the material—that is, with the selvedge threads running from the top to the bottom of the garment. This would be so in every article of clothing, if cut out properly.

Narrow hems, about one-sixth inch, are needed on either side of the opening. These hems require the utmost care in fixing, as they should taper off to the extreme point of the slit; consequently the hems must be well flattened with the left thumbnail, in order to stretch the calico to ensure its flatness. The slightest bit of pucker depreciates the work.

Fig. 77 shows the hems fixed, which gives the opening a U shaped appearance. It is not necessary to hem these folds until the tape is put on, and then the material left over after the tape is arranged can be hemmed.

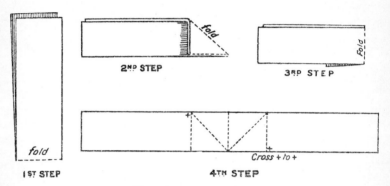

FIG. 78.—PREPARATION OF THE TAPE.

To Prepare the Tape.—A piece of tape about 3¼ in. in length, and about ⅜ in. width, is suitable for most garments. For fine material it may be a little narrower. In order to make the tape *set well*, it is necessary to " cross or twist it," and in consequence it is sometimes called a " shaped " tape, to distinguish it from the *straight* piece of tape which is frequently felled over the raw edges on the wrong side of openings in garments, when arranged with one hem stitched across another hem.

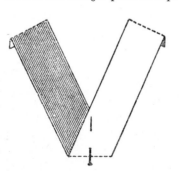

FIG. 79.—APPEARANCE OF THE PREPARED TAPE.

Fold the tape as follows (Fig. 78)—

1. Double the tape in half as shown in the diagram, and make a crease across its width (1st step).

2. Bend down the folded corner to make a diagonal crease (2nd step).

3. Fold under the tape from the top of the diagonal crease so as to make a creased square (3rd step).

4. Open out the tape flat (4th step) and cross the *bottom right*-hand corner of one square to the *top left*-hand corner of the other, and put a pin in the twist to hold it firmly. (Fig. 79.) Turn under the narrow raw edges of the tape once (*see* Fig. 79), and the little projecting corners may be cut off, or they will tuck under nicely with the needle.

Expert workers should fold this tape (the angle is about 60°) without the aid of the creases.

To Arrange the Tape—

1. The tape should be placed on to the wrong side, with the *point* of the V of the tape *to the bottom of the hem* (*C* in Fig. 77), and the pin already in use will serve to keep the tape fixed.

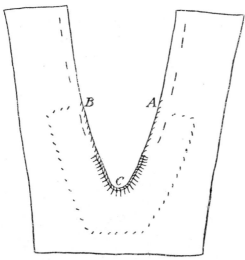

FIG. 80.—TAPE COMPLETE ON THE RIGHT SIDE.

2. If preferred, the edge of the tape *may be tacked* to the folded edge of the hem, but so small a piece of work easily admits of working without tacking. Turn the material representing the garment to the right side, and hold it so that the *slit opening is towards the right hand.* Hold the *near side* of the garment and tape between the thumb and finger. Begin to sew at *A* in Fig. 80, and work all round to *B*, putting close stitches at *C*. Do not break the cotton. Stroke the sewing to make the work quite flat.

3. Turn the work to the wrong side, and the cotton will be in readiness to fell down the edge of the tape on the wrong side. It is, perhaps, better to tack this, but is optional. The fold of crossed tape at the bottom will need stretching

to make the tape set perfectly flat on the material. The turned-in corners will slant as in the diagram. Fell round as far as D, Fig. 81, making the stitches show through regularly. The little piece of cross tape at D must be felled (it is better not to let the stitches show on the right side), and when finished the needle can be slipped between the tape and the material to D, and the felling resumed. The finishing off should be neat and strong, and the end slipped between. Flatten the felling well.

4. The bottom of the slit and the edge of the tape should be button-holed (*see* Figs. 60 and 61). Hold the *right* side towards the worker. Slip the needle between the folds, and bring it out at the edge nearly half an inch to the left of *C*. Work the stitch rather close and tightly, about $\frac{1}{10}$ in. deep, and extend the working to the same distance from *C* on the right-hand side. Fasten off similarly to the commencement.

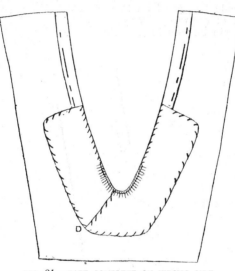

FIG. 81.—TAPE COMPLETE ON WRONG SIDE.

This button-holing is not absolutely necessary, but lends a neat finish.

III. Remarks.—A large piece of very coarse linen and tape or ribbon (about an inch in width), with coloured thread, provide the best means of illustrating this lesson to a class. Tape can be tinted to contrast with material. (Dyes cost very little and are obtainable at all general stores.)

IV. Faults likely to occur—

1. Badly-fixed hem on the material representing the garment.

2. Tape not an even length on either side of the opening—caused by the tape being prepared incorrectly.

4. Stitches badly shaped.

5. Puckering at the bottom of the opening.

CHAPTER XVI

INSERTION OF A GUSSET

I. Definition and Use.—A gusset is a piece of material inserted into a garment, generally a shirt or drawers, in order to prevent a seam or opening from splitting where there is likely to be any strain, and also to give a neat finish to a garment.

It is one of those dainty little pieces of needlework which give opportunity for the worker to stamp her own individuality upon the process. Being a small piece of work it requires most skilful handling, and pays well for a careful study of method. It also gives good practice in awkward portions of the elementary stitches, viz., hemming, sewing, and stitching, and taken as a whole, shows up good teaching to such an extent as to prove a complete success, or almost a failure.

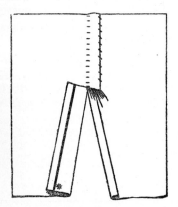

FIG. 82.—
* *The material to the left of the thick line should be cut away.*

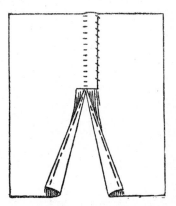

FIG. 83.—OPENING PREPARED AS ON THE WRONG SIDE.

II. Preparation of Material.—The seam (either run-and-fell, or sew-and-fell) where the gusset is to be inserted will be the selvedge way of the material, *i.e.*, if the garment has been cut out properly ; therefore, for practice purposes, the pieces of material representing the garment must be torn *selvedge* way, and joined (for an inch or two only) by a sew-and-fell or run-and-fell seam (this means that the sewing and felling must be worked *parallel with the selvedge threads*). The turnings of the material should be narrow, so that the whole seam is not more than ⅛ in. when complete. The felling should be finished off about *two* stitches ($\frac{1}{8}$ in.) short of the place where the sewing ended. The reason

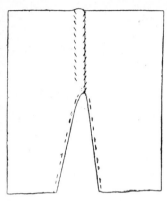

FIG. 84.—OPENING PREPARED AS ON THE RIGHT SIDE.

for this will be seen when the gusset is inserted, as the felling of the gusset will appear as a continuation of the felling of the seam. (Fig. 87.) The sides of the material extending from the seam will require turning with narrow hems, which should taper off gradually to the end of the seam. The gusset may be put in before these folds are hemmed, then the material not covered by the gusset can be worked after the gusset is completed. In order to make a gusset set perfectly flat at the point (and this is very essential) it will be necessary to snip across the entire *fell* upon the wrong side, just at right angles to the *end of the sewing* (**not** *the felling*), *and not a fraction of an inch beyond it.* Flatten out the material which formed the fell, and in order to facilitate the turnings of the hems and enable the gusset to set flatly at the point of insertion, the *whole of the first turn* of what formed the fell should be sloped away. The hems, which are to be *tacked only*, should be very narrow, turned *quite into a point at the sewing*, and thoroughly well flattened. All raw edges will be covered by the gusset on the wrong side, and the right side should present a perfectly flat and tidy appearance. Figs. 82, 83, and 84 will illustrate each step.

A teacher should provide herself with a paper, or a coarse material specimen, upon which to illustrate each portion of the work.

The class might turn a paper gusset preparatory to the calico one.

If striped cutting-out paper be used, and one of the sides of the square be cut straight by a line, the way of the threads and the stretching peculiarities of the *material* gusset, owing to the method of cutting, can be easily shown to advantage.

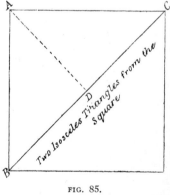

FIG. 85.

III. Preparation of the Gusset.—Gussets are always in pairs, *e.g.*, at the wrist, armhole, or hip. A square of material is sufficient to make a pair. Hip or side gussets are rather larger than those put into a sleeve. A wrist gusset is sufficiently small if cut from a 3 in. square. Fig. 85 shows a square of material, which, if cut diagonally, gives two isosceles triangles. Fig. 86 illustrates each step in progress. A = apex; BC = base line. Make a crease down the centre, extending from the apex to the base—AD. Turn a narrow fold on to the wrong side, barely $\frac{1}{8}$ in. all round the triangle, the base first. Press the corners well. Fig. 86 (1st step).

Keep the raw edges facing the worker. Fold down the apex A on to the centre crease, till it barely touches the *raw edge* of the turning of the base. (Fig. 86, 2nd step.) Crease across EF. Turn up the corners B, C to meet E, F *exactly* (be sure these ends fold down quite flatly — the corners can be held with the thumb and finger, and the scissors' blade inserted between the folds to make the material flat) and *cut off* the little corners even with the *other turnings* of the gusset and *not at the fold*. (Fig. 86, 3rd step.) The triangle EAF will be part of the gusset seen on the right side, and the hexagon will be on the wrong.

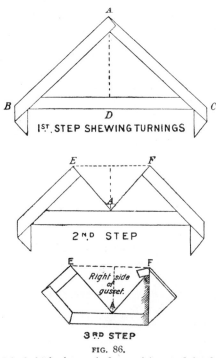

FIG. 86.

Only the left-hand corner is shown as being cut off, but the right-hand one is left turned up so as to show C touching F.

IV. Directions for Insertion—

1. Hold the *right* side of the garment towards the worker with the seam to the *left* hand, and the opening to the *right*.

2. Place point A of the gusset *exactly* to the end of the sewing, holding the edge of the garment and the gusset firmly in place between the thumb and finger. The work is handled more freely without tacking, but if preferred, a few loose stitches may secure point A.

3. Begin to sew at crease F, make a few strong stitches at A, and sew round to E on the other side—*do not break cotton*—

flatten the sewing well, as it cannot be done conveniently afterwards.

4. Turn the work to the wrong side, and pin the perpendicular crease of the gusset *exactly to the sewing*. Fell all round as far as the pin, pulling up the corner so that the *sides are true to a right angle, and parallel with the weft and selvedge threads of the material*—this is very essential as the corner has a tendency to slant. The felling is most awkward, and every care must be taken to make the stitches regular and the correct shape. It will be necessary to slightly stretch the base in order to make the gusset set flat, as upon this flatness its beauty depends—remove the pin and place it at the unworked corner, *which must be pulled up into position*

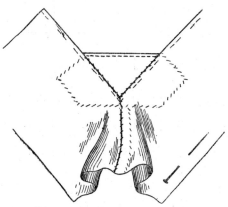

FIG. 87.—GUSSET COMPLETE ON RIGHT SIDE.

to match the opposite side—*stretch* the base to match the half already worked (at this stage it must be noticed if a sufficient length of felling of the seam has been done), and complete the felling of the gusset—*do not break off the cotton*.

5. Turn the work to the right side—stitch the folded edge of gusset *close to its edge* ($\frac{1}{10}$ in. below) to flatten it, and give a general finish.

It will be seen that there is no occasion to make joining of cotton at the corners if the work be held and started as directed.

Figs. 87 and 88 show the gusset complete on both the right and wrong sides.

If a gusset be put into a run-and-fell seam, the *right* side of garment and the *right* side of gusset will be held together, so that the wrong side of the garment must face the worker, which will bring the sewing on the wrong side ; the other working is the same.

A gusset of *single* material may be put under the arm of a baby's short-coating shirt. In this case, the straight sides are stitched into the armhole, and the side on the cross slightly shaped and hemmed round with the other part of the sleeve.

A gusset may be put into the side opening of a child's drawers. In this case, the hems at the sides of the vent should be turned to a point. The gusset can then be inserted as described above. The point requires care (as there is *no seam* at which to place it), and may need a few stitches of button-holing at the apex on the right side.

V. Faults for Criticism are—

1. Badly prepared opening into which the gusset is to be inserted.

2. Gusset not geometrical in shape, and unevenly turned— *corners not cut off.*

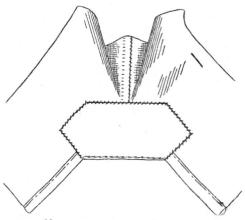

FIG. 88.—GUSSET COMPLETE ON WRONG SIDE.

3. Gusset clumsily inserted on the right side—point not being put to the seam, and the sides unequally sewn as regards length.

4. Wrong side irregular in appearance—a larger portion of gusset on one side of the seam than on the other—*sides not parallel with the threads of the material,* so that the corners do not form a right angle.

5. Felling not forming a protection to the point on the right side—caused by the gusset not being prepared as shown in Fig. 86.

6. Fastenings not secure, and corners untidy.

7. General appearance not flat.

N.B. Stitching, seaming, and felling stitches to be criticised as described in those chapters.

VI. Remarks.—A gusset is sometimes made from a square of material, in which case a triangle would appear on the wrong side as well as the right. The method described in detail is the more general.

CHAPTER XVII

FEATHER, CORAL OR TREE STITCH—KNOTTING OR SEEDING

I. Introduction.—This stitch is probably so named from its resemblance to the barbs of a feather, the branches of coral, or the twigs of a tree.

It is really a branch of fancy work, but in plain needlework it is used in place of stitching, and is a great saving of time, labour and eyesight. Hand stitching has now almost disappeared in the making of garments, and feather-stitching has largely taken its place as an ornament to garments intended for women and children, and if *well* worked, it is difficult to name a more effective and inexpensive means of decorating underclothing. It is very essential that the general rules for working be observed, otherwise, if the stitches are coarse and irregular, it takes from, rather than adding to, the beauty of a garment ; and it is never advisable to ornament garments in which the elementary stitches, such as hemming, sewing, gathering, etc., are not creditably worked.

II. Use.—In plain needlework this stitch is used for ornamentation upon neckbands, wristbands, fronts of garments, etc.

In fancy work it is one of the fundamental stitches.

III. Materials for Working.—The stitch may be taught upon flannel similar to that employed for teaching herring-boning, but frequently other material is preferred for the initiatory steps. Various kinds of threads are used for the stitch, each of which has its advantages.

Feather-stitching should not be worked with ordinary sewing cotton, nor cotton which is too thick in comparison with the texture of the material.

1. **Crochet Cotton** is generally used, and always looks well. It is very strong wearing, but, unfortunately, it often becomes a bad colour in washing. No. 18, 20, or 22 are good sizes for medium longcloth or cambric.

2. **Flax, or Flourishing Thread,** such as is used for mending house and table linen.

This is very suitable upon fine material, mull muslin, cambric, etc., as the thread is soft and glossy, and crochet cotton would be more harsh looking.

For garments subjected to hard wear, flax thread is not to be recommended, as it soon breaks with hard rubbing in frequent washing, although it keeps its colour well.

3. **Embroidery Cotton,** to be had in several sizes, is another suitable thread for a material that is not glossy It is exceedingly soft to work with, and wears admirably.

4. **Wool, Yarn, or Silk** may be used for flannel or stuff garments. Flannel silk keeps its colour in washing and is unshrinkable, and wears much better than the many common substitutes which have been manufactured in recent years. several of which are hardly worth using. Filoselle, crewel silk, and flax thread are sometimes used upon flannel. Andalusian wool, orbest quality fingering yarn, is also recommended.

A crewel or embroidery needle should be used which will carry the thread easily, but not any coarser than is necessary, otherwise holes are made in the material. A No. 6 or 7 sewing needle will carry crochet cotton, but a darning needle is most awkward to use.

FIG. 89.— COMMENCEMENT OF FEATHER- STITCHING.

A long length of thread should not be taken, as speed is retarded and wool or silk is liable to get impoverished ; 24 in. is a suitable length.

IV. Description of the Stitch.—Feather-stitching should consist of stitches (one, two, or three) worked alternately right and left of an *imaginary* centre line. The material should be held over the fingers as for hemming.

To Commence.—Bring the needle through to the right side, leaving a finger length of cotton hanging, which can be darned in when the work is finished—bend the thread round to the right hand, making half a loop as shown in Fig. 89—place the thumb upon the loop—insert the needle a little to the right just above the place where the cotton comes out, taking up a *small* piece of material and slanting the needle slightly toward the left—still keep the thumb upon the cotton, taking care that the needle is *above* the thread which forms the loop—draw through gently toward the worker, but not loosing the thumb till the cotton is almost home. Bend the thread to the left, making half a loop as before—insert the needle a little to the left just above the place where the cotton comes out, and take up another small piece of material—draw the needle out as on the other side—continue working thus, the stitches radiating alternately right and left. To fasten off, pass the needle to the wrong side, and run along under the stitches already worked. Thread needle with the end left at the commencement, and treat in the same way.

This is known as " single " feather-stitching. The " double " is worked in the same manner, only two stitches to the right and left alternately ; sometimes three to left and three to right are chosen. The needle for the new stitch must always be put in a little above the level of the bottom of the preceding one.

V. The Stitch upon Calico.—If feather-stitching be worked on a band, it will be the *selvedge* way and on double material—if between tucks, as for a chemise or nightgown, it is always *selvedge* way and on *single* material—if on a hem at the bottom of a garment, it is *weft* way—if at the neck, it may be on the *cross* of the material if the band is so arranged. Feather-stitching may be worked anywhere and at any part of a garment, if consistent with good judgment.

A thread must not be drawn for the purpose of keeping the stitch straight; but a crease, a line of tacking, a mark scratched with the needle, may all be used as a guide for regularity; but Nature's guide, viz., a correct eye for gauging distances, is the best assistant.

To Commence.—The stitch should never be commenced with a KNOT. If the material is double as in a band, the thread can always be slipped *between the folds*, but on single material the needle should be brought through from the wrong side, and a length of thread should be left hanging which can be held down with the left forefinger, and worked in with the first few stitches so as to secure it, or the needle may be threaded with this end when the work is finished, and it can then be run under the other stitches. Knots are as unnecessary as they are unsightly, but inexperienced workers frequently use knots, and in consequence lose many marks for neatness and daintiness of general finish.

All stitches should be uniform in size and show a continuity from one stitch to the next.

IT IS ALMOST IMPOSSIBLE TO WORK FEATHER-STITCHING TOO CLOSE OR TOO SMALL FOR "GOOD STYLE."

A VERY (this cannot be expressed too emphatically) small piece of material must be taken on the needle (not more than $\frac{1}{10}$ or $\frac{1}{12}$ of an in.).

The cotton should not be pulled *in the least degree tightly*; in fact, it should look as though it were "laid on" (appliqué) to the material—not "woven in." In order that the stitch may appear compact, the needle must be inserted *half-way* up the length of the last stitch, and *not on a line* with the place from which the cotton hangs, which quite spoils the raised effect of otherwise good work. (Half-way up the length of the last stitch is shown in Fig. 90 by small dots.)

The appearance of the stitches is much improved if the needle be slightly slanted alternately towards the right and left; *e.g.*, when working the *right*-hand stitches slant the needle to the *left*, and when working the *left*-hand slant the needle to the *right*. (Fig. 90.)

There is a tendency to *increase* the size of the stitches as the work proceeds, which must be avoided, as compactness is very essential.

To Join.—If working on double material, the needle can be passed to the wrong side *just underneath*, *i.e.*, below the V or U

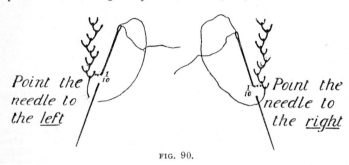

FIG. 90.

formed by the last stitch, and the needle can then be slipped between the folds, before being *cut* off—the cotton should never be snapped.

Fig. 91 shows the appearance of the cotton when fastened off on the right and wrong sides.

If working on single material, the cotton must be run under the previously worked stitches on the wrong side.

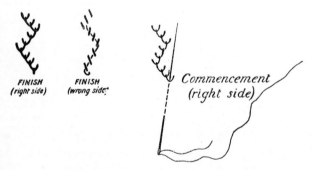

FIG. 91.—SHOWING A JOIN IN FEATHER-STITCHING.

The commencement with the new thread is the same as when starting the work, the needle being brought out *exactly* in the loop which was formed by the last stitch, either by slipping between the fold of the material or leaving the end hanging and working it in with the new stitches, according as required for single or double material. (Fig. 91.)

The join will be almost invisible on the right side, and firm and neat on the wrong.

Fig. 92 shows " single," " double," and " treble " feather-stitching.

In ornamenting the front of any garment, the feather-stitching should always be started *from the neck and worked downwards* (there is a tendency to work downwards one side of the front and upwards on the other).

For turning a corner, as from a neckband to the front of a garment, if intending to work to the right hand, make the *last* stitch of the old side and *first* stitch of the new on the right hand of the centre line ; if turning to the left hand, make the *last* and *first* stitch on the *left* hand of the centre.

FIG. 92.

Feather-stitching to be good must be *absolutely* spotless. Crochet cotton shows soil very quickly. The fingers need to be scrupulously clean for working this stitch, as the slightest soil depreciates any specimen of work. The finger tips can be frequently freshened by rubbing a small quantity of cotton between them, which has the effect of smoothing them at the same time. Children should be allowed to freshen the fingers frequently in this way; the small waste of cotton is nothing compared with the benefits to be derived from cleanly worked garments.

VI. Remarks.—A distinction (with but a slight difference) is sometimes drawn between " feather " stitch and " coral " stitch. If worked with straight stitches it is known as " coral " stitch, but as " feather-stitching " if a slanting stitch be produced.

An exceedingly pretty ornamentation for trimming fine and dainty underclothing, where " lace " insertion (Torchon or Valenciennes) can be used, is made by working feather-stitching on *very narrow* ($\frac{1}{4}$ in.) *linen* tape (common twilled cotton tape is not worth using). Linen tape of this width is inexpensive, and if worked as suggested and sewn between the strips of insertion it makes a very effective trimming. This may provide a suggestion for some holiday needlework to those anxious for something small and useful.

VII. Points for Criticism are—

1. The use of unsuitable material and thread for working purposes.

2. The stitch wrongly applied and in an unfit place on the garment. Feather-stitching should not be worked *over* another stitch, *e.g.*, hemming or running.

3. Incorrect method of forming the stitch, and slanting *from* the centre instead of *towards* it.

4. Size of stitches out of proportion to the threads of the material.

5. Irregular and uneven distances between the stitches.

6. Insecure, untidy, and clumsy joins—KNOTS.

7. Thread drawn too tightly, and so producing a puckered appearance.

8. General want of uniformity and compactness, owing to lack of practice, and inability to gauge space.

KNOTTING OR SEEDING.

I. Introduction.—In plain needlework, knotting is entirely an ornamental stitch. It is used in conjunction with coral stitch, as a means of decorating any garment, especially baby linen. It is a stitch largely and effectively used in embroidery for filling in the seed vessels in the centres of flowers, also for working clusters of berries. In fancy work the stitches are called French knots and are worked in a slightly different way, but the same in principle.

The same materials as recommended for feather-stitching would be suitable for knotting. If a large knot be needed, it is advisable to use coarser thread or to double the strands, as this will give a firmer knot than would be made by twisting the thread several times around the needle.

II. Method of Forming the Knot—

1. Hold the material as for hemming.

2. Bring the needle through to the right side.

3. Make a loop (close to where the cotton comes out) from left to right, about as big as a threepenny piece. Let the long end of the cotton go to the left. Hold the point of the thumb upon the loop.

4. Take a small piece of material (say $\frac{1}{10}$ in.), bringing the needle out where the cotton came from in the first instance. (Fig. 93.)

5. Pass the needle *over* the long end of cotton, and lift the loop up *on* the needle, either from the centre or from underneath the left-hand side of the loop and up through the centre.

6. Draw through rather smartly upwards, towards the ceiling.

7. Insert the needle again in the place where the stitch was made, and bring out just in front of the place where the next knot is wanted.

III. Knots Applied.—Knots are sometimes worked in conjunction with double or treble coral stitch, the knots being put in the interspaces between the vandykes of the stitches.

FIG. 93

Knotting may be used alone as an ornament, according to the discretion of the worker and the character of the work in hand. If working upon double material, always slip the needle between the fold when passing from stitch to stitch. This makes the wrong side much neater, and is stronger for washing purposes. Care must be taken not to pucker the material. The ends of cotton may be fastened as described in feather-stitching.

IV. Remarks.—Good knotting consists of firm even knots, at regularly placed distances apart, suitable in size to the material, neat on the wrong side and with an absence of any puckering.

CHAPTER XVIII

BINDING FLANNEL

I. Introduction.—Binding is a term used in plain needlework to denote the neatening of the edge of any material by covering it with folded ribbon, tape, or braid, so as to protect and strengthen the edge, and at the same time to keep the garment flat and neat.

Flannel Binding, or galloon, is a thin, silky kind of ribbon, used to neaten the raw edge of flannel. Binding can be bought in widths, varying from ⅜ to ¾ in. The widths are known in the trade as 2d., 4d., 6d., 8d., 10d., the thickness of the old penny coins being taken as the standard (½ in. is the best width for use on garments). It is not considered an easy task to bind flannel *well*, and some practice is necessary in order to produce work which presents a *perfectly flat* appearance on both binding and flannel.

Machine silk should be used for both working and tacking.

II. Method of Binding.—Keep the right side of the flannel uppermost, and begin with the selvedge side. Turn down a fold of the binding, about one-third or one-fourth of its depth, and the right side on to the wrong, if there should be a distinction.

Leave a small margin of binding in starting (to be cut even afterwards), as it always frays. Place the raw edges of the flannel *well up* into the fold of the binding, and fix very carefully near the edge of the binding, but not so as to be in the way of the stitches in working. In order to keep the binding *very flat* (and this is *most* essential), it is necessary to slightly ease in the flannel (and rather more on a weft edge than a selvedge) and to hold the binding *very* tightly, otherwise it will arrange itself in little flutes, and it must set perfectly flat *when* the hands have relaxed their hold.

Every care is necessary to avoid pulling the threads of the binding " out of the upright." The ridges should be kept perfectly at *right angles to their own edges* on both sides. There is a tendency to strain the wrong side, so that the threads are pushed out of the straight, upright position ; and as they easily slant, constant care is necessary in working, as if they once get slanted nothing will right them but re-working the entire side.

Turning a corner needs very skilful handling (it should be practised on paper till the " knack " of turning *sharply* is acquired) as the corner must be a *perfect right angle*, which is formed as follows : Tack the binding *quite up close to the raw edges of the adjacent side*, and grip the binding at this edge between the *right*-hand thumb and finger—bend the work round (still gripping) and with the left-hand thumb and finger fold down the second side of the binding, and by using just the tip of the needle the diagonal corner will fix itself in place on both sides, the right side fold falling towards the *right hand*, and the wrong side fold towards the *left hand*. If a square is being bound, the fourth corner must be arranged to match the others, thus : Cut the binding of the first side even with the flannel, and also cut the fourth side, but allowing $\frac{1}{4}$ in. to turn under. The corners must be bent under with the needle to make a diagonal on both sides.

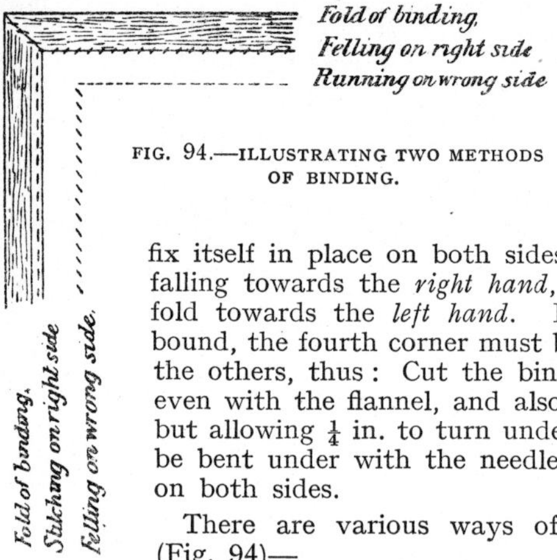

Fold of binding.
Felling on right side
Running on wrong side

FIG. 94.—ILLUSTRATING TWO METHODS OF BINDING.

Fold of binding.
Stitching on right side.
Felling on wrong side.

There are various ways of securing the edges (Fig. 94)—

1. *Felling* on the right side and running on the wrong. (The most practical, and recommended for garments.)

2. *Felling* on both sides.

3. *Stitching* on the right side, and running on the wrong. (This looks very neat, and is not difficult to work, as the ridges of the binding so easily regulate the size of the stitches.

4. *Stitching* on the right side and felling on the wrong) The stitches on the *right* side should not show through on the wrong, or else *every* stitch should show. With stitching, it is difficult to avoid taking the stitches through, and the wrong side of the binding is often held up out of the way with the forefinger. (Some experienced workers prefer to tack the binding flat, then work the right side and fold down the wrong afterwards.)

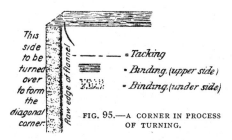

This side to be turned over to form the diagonal corner

Raw edge of flannel

- - - - - = *Tacking*
▬ = *Binding. (upper side)*
▓ = *Binding. (under side)*

FIG. 95.—A CORNER IN PROCESS OF TURNING.

When working the corners the diagonals are sometimes felled, and the best way of arranging is to *slip the needle up to the corner* and fell down to the edge, so as to continue the side. If working round a curve, the binding must be eased to keep its flatness as much as possible.

Fig. 95 shows a corner in process of turning.

III. Points for Criticism are—

1. Binding not forming sufficient protection to the edge of the flannel (a common fault)—uneven fixing.

2. Binding threads strained out of the vertical line on the wrong side.

3. Stitches badly formed, irregular, and too closely worked —joins insecure—corners not a right angle.

4. Binding or flannel drawn or puckered, and the general appearance showing unskilful handling.

CHAPTER XIX

WHIPPING AND SETTING ON A FRILL

I. Introduction.—Hand-made frilling has fallen into disuse of late years, probably because so many kinds of patent trimmings have been introduced, which answer the purpose equally as well for ornament, and take considerably less time to set on.

In the days of our grandmothers, education in needlework would not have been considered complete unless proficiency had been attained in whipping, which was so much approved of in those times ; but there are many good needlewomen who still think highly of whipping as testing the skill of a seamstress, yet it is sometimes difficult to induce teachers to realise the educational value of the stitch, which affords a finger training and gives a manipulative power unequalled by any other process of work. Every one will allow that to hem, whip, and set on a frill, requires a dexterity with the fingers not possessed by every one, and it certainly is the stitch *par excellence* as a test of ability. It is not that the " whip " and setting-on stitch is difficult, but that fine material in a small quantity has to be dealt with, and this requires a good amount of handling. There are certainly quicker ways of trimming garments, but the " whip " stitch may be put to other uses than that of trimming underclothing.

II. Material necessary.—*Fine* mull muslin, nainsook, or cambric are the best kinds of material to use for ornamenting calico or longcloths. The above materials vary in width from 36 to 43 inches. The cheaper qualities will not tear without dragging the threads, and are not to be recommended for frills. *Linen lawn* (40 in. wide) is an exceedingly fine material, and is only suitable for the daintiest garments. Mercerized lawn is a very good material for teaching purposes : it is thin, and the edge can be rolled easily. Cotton No. 100 should be used for hemming the frill, and No. 60 for the whipping and setting on the frill to the band.

III. Preparation of Material.—Frilling *must be torn weft* way of the material, *i.e.*, with the selvedge the short way or the depth of the frill, else it cannot easily be rolled for whipping, and sets very badly when put on to garments. It is better to tear the frills the required width, and cut off the fluffy edge before hemming or whipping. The width of the frill is a matter of taste ; slightly less than ¾ in., *when complete*, is a suitable width. This will necessitate cutting the frill about an inch. Frills, from 3 to 6 in., are often used now as trimming for underclothing. These frills are intended to fall down over the garment. A narrow frill would stand upright.

The proportion of frilling to the band is usually *twice* the length ; sometimes a little more is allowed to give extra fulness (say, $2\frac{1}{4}$ times the length of the band). If more frilling is needed than the width of muslin will allow, the garment must be measured and the required length must be joined, *before* hemming or whipping, either by sewing selvedges (which are generally even in muslin), or by a *very narrow* run-and-fell. For a circular band for the wrists, armholes, or knees, the frill must be joined to form a round *before beginning to hem or whip it.*

IV. Hem of Frill.—This should be as narrow as it is possible for fingers to make it—*never* more than $\frac{3}{8}$ of an inch. It is sometimes made with just the edge rolled under and then hemmed. The short sides of the frill should be hemmed *before* the fold for the hem is turned, and the corners neatly sewn up. The edge should be trimmed of fluff just before turning the hem ; it will be necessary to turn nearly as much for the first time as for the second. The hemming stitches should not be close, but uniform and regular.

After the hemming is completed, the half and quarters must be marked to correspond with the band of the garment ; this is very essential in order to secure regularity in setting-on.

V. Directions for Making the Roll and Working the Whip-stitch.—It is needless to remark that *scrupulously* clean fingers are necessary for this process, as the slightest soil depreciates the work ; and, though the hands may be quite fresh, it is as well to rub some sewing cotton between the finger tips before starting the rolling.

FIG. 96.

Fig. 96 illustrates the direction and slant of the stitch and the proportion between stitch and space.

Trim the edge to be whipped just before beginning to whip, as any frayings will add to the coarseness of the roll, and the aim should be to keep this as *neat and tight as possible*. Coarser cotton is needed than that used for the hemming, as the material is required to be drawn up, and so a strain is put upon it ; and the cotton must be threaded with *the end which hangs from the reel*, and not the one broken from the bulk of the cotton (there is an inclination to thread this end), which rubs the fibres of the cotton the wrong way.

The whip-stitch is worked thus—

1. Hold the *wrong* side of the frill to the worker, in a position somewhat as for sewing, the raw edge being uppermost.

2. Work from *right to left*. With the thumb and finger of the right hand turn down the tiniest hem possible at the right-hand corner (or if a circular piece of frilling is in hand, begin at the join), and on the fold secure the cotton as for hemming.

3. Assistance is given to the rolling if the material which is in the left palm be kept at a moderately tight tension by the third and fourth fingers. With an *upwards* and downwards gentle motion of the left thumb commence a neat, tight roll; and as the thumb passes downwards, draw it gently *towards the left*, and so bring it off the roll, but be sure that the raw edge is completely hidden. Breathing on the fingers is not a cleanly habit, but is frequently done to assist the rolling. It should be avoided as much as possible.

FIG. 97.—WHIPPING IN PROGRESS.

4. Roll about an inch at a time. Insert the needle *from the back*, *i.e.*, from the *right* side of the frill, being that part which is against the forefinger, and bring the needle out pointing slantingly towards the chest, *just under the roll*. (Fig. 100.)

The needle is put in *as for sewing, only in a slanting direction*, and the stitches are made barely $\frac{1}{8}$ in. apart.

The distance between each stitch must be gauged by the eye when a start is made. It is as well to roll only as much material as a few stitches will cover, as the roll must be kept tight.

The worked frill can be held *round* the first finger to steady it.

The material should be moved along the thread every inch or two, to make sure the roll has not been caught, as if so, the frill will not draw, and the thread will break.

Do not draw up too closely (not closer than is needed for the band) or the frill will get twisted, as it is very inclined to do this.

5. Leave the cotton hanging at the end of the frill. If a quantity of frilling is needed, it will be necessary to take new cotton at the half and quarters. Leave the thread hanging as for gathering, and commence the new cotton with a few backstitches on the wrong side just under the roll.

If the above directions have been followed, the roll will be divided into little ridges or curls, slanting from the *right towards the left* (Fig. 97), the stitches lying between the curl, in each groove or furrow.

The work reduces itself to three stages: (1) Rolling, (2) Whipping, and (3) Testing the work by drawing it up.

For good work, only one stitch should be taken at a time, as this ensures a smaller ridge to each whip; but for quickness, and for whipping lace, as many stitches may be taken upon the needle as it will hold; in fact, a milliner would not draw the needle throughout the length, but as it becomes full, slip the work on to the cotton.

VI. Directions for Setting on the Frill to the Band.—(Fig. 98.) The curls of the frill will be attached to the *folded* edge of band.

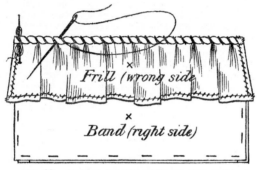

FIG. 98.—SETTING ON THE FRILL TO THE BAND.

The band must be prepared and tacked as described in Chapter V.

Hold the *right* side of the band to the worker, and place the right side of the frill to face it. Pin the halves and quarters, and distribute the fulness evenly, securing the cotton around a small pin. Fixing threads may be put in if desired, but pinning (with small pins) usually answers the purpose. Hold the material in the same position as for sewing, with the frill facing the worker. Secure the cotton as if about to sew. Insert the needle so that it catches up the *extreme edge of the fold of the band*, and passes through the *left-hand end* of the curl of the whip in a *slanting* direction. The setting-on stitch will then fall *in the groove or furrow* between each ridge.

The diagram will help to make this clearer. (Fig. 98.)

The fullness can be regulated with the needle as the work proceeds. Do not pull the stitches too tightly, or the thread will break when the frill is flattened from the band. It will be seen that the whipping thread and the sewing thread both run in the *same* direction, viz., from right to left. Fasten off the whipping thread by hemming the rolled-under-edge to match the beginning (the raw edges should be cut off). The setting-on cotton should be fastened by sewing back a few stitches. The frill must be well flattened from the band.

The appearance of the frill is improved if it be *very gently* stroked with the needle after flattening.

A deep frill, intended to fall over the shoulders, would be set-on on the right side; in this case, place the *right* side of the frill to the *wrong* side of the band.

Fig. 99 shows the frill complete.

FIG. 99.

VII. Remarks.—Some people set on a frill while holding the *band* towards the worker; the same result is obtained, but it is more difficult to regulate the fullness, as the whipping thread is at the right hand instead of the left. It would be necessary, if this plan were followed, to draw the frill up exactly to the length of the band, and fasten off the whipping thread before setting on. Great care is needed to distribute the fullness evenly, and it is not recommended, as the liability to break the thread is so great. It seems more natural, however, to hold any full-ness towards the worker, and the majority of good workers prefer to teach it in this way. Whipping is an exceedingly neat and quick way of gathering lace. Embroidery is sometimes whipped before setting on to a band. This lends a pretty effect to the trimming, especially if the material on which the embroidery is worked is of a soft texture.

VIII. Features in which the Working of Whipping and Gathering are similar—

1. The material is prepared *weft* way of the muslin.

2. The same proportion of material to band is allowed.

3. The work is halved and quartered to secure regularity.

4. The drawing-up thread is left unfastened while setting into, or on a band, and secured at the finish.

5. Each little ruck or fullness receives a stitch in attaching it to the band.

6. Gathers and frills are fastened to a band with a stitch peculiar to each, requiring a certain position of the needle.

IX. Faults likely to occur—

1. Badly prepared frill—made selvedge way of the stuff — hem too broad—ends untidy.

2. Roll of frill too coarse and loose, irregular and clumsy.

3. Incorrect stitch in whipping. Sometimes a " roll hem " is formed by inserting the needle from the front as for hemming ; the curls then slope from *left to right*, and cannot be set on properly. (*See* Note.)

4. Whipping thread too tight, not allowing the material to draw up, or else so loose that a coarse, ugly ridge is the result.

5. Frilling not evenly distributed along the band.

6. Incorrect slope to the setting-on stitch. Each groove should have its own thread lying in it.

7. Cotton pulled too tightly in setting-on.

8. Insecure fastenings and untidy joins.

9. An unfinished and general clumsy appearance, through want of practice in the art of handling work, deficiency of finger skill, and a lack of delicacy in dealing with dainty materials.

NOTE.—" Roll hemming " is frequently used in elaborately made underclothing when it is required to join plain material to a lace insertion. The work is held *flat over* the fingers—the material is rolled and the stitch secures the rolled edge, and, at the same time, is passed into the extreme edge of the insertion, which is laid flat over the fingers to the left of the rolled edge.

CHAPTER XX

DIFFERENT METHODS OF MAKING SEAMS IN GARMENTS

I. A Sew-and-Fell.—Described in Chapter IV.

II. A Run-and-Fell.—Described in Chapter XIV.

III. A Mantua-maker's or Hemmed Seam.—This is sometimes used on fine material, such as muslin or cambric. No stitches are seen on the right side, but a ridge of material is unavoidable on the wrong. It is a quick method of joining material for frocks or pinafores, as one set of stitches suffices to keep the seam firm. It is worked as follows: Place the right sides of material together, the front raw edge just a trifle (barely $\frac{1}{10}$ in.) below the back. Fold both edges over together as for an ordinary hem

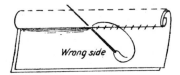

FIG. 100.—A MANTUA-MAKER'S SEAM.

(narrow), and then hem *through the double material*, taking the stitches well through to the reverse side. Fig. 100 shows the seam flattened down in process of hemming. No stitches will be visible on the right side.

IV. A French Seam (so-called).—This is another method of joining material, which makes both right and wrong sides neat. (Figs. 101 and 102.) It is worked thus: Place the two *wrong* sides of the material together, the raw edges being perfectly even. At a distance of about $\frac{1}{8}$ in. from the edge, lightly run the two pieces of material together. Cut off any fluffy edge, and turn the material to the *wrong* side, so that the right sides are facing. Press the join well between the thumb and finger, so that it may come quite at the edge. Tack firmly and run-stitch (or *run* only if very thin material) nearly a $\frac{1}{4}$ in. from the joined edge, or so as quite to clear the turned-in edges. Be very careful that the frayings of *the raw edges do not show through on the right side*. This kind of seam is often used for muslin and print frocks, and pinafores.

It is a kind of seam easily produced by machining, and is

one of the most secure, but it leaves a ridge on the wrong side, so is found to be slightly bulky.

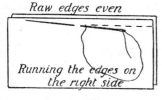
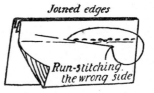

FIG. 101.   FIG. 102.

A FRENCH SEAM.

V. Counter Hemming.—This is another way of joining two pieces of material, in which hemming stitches are worked on both *right* and *wrong* sides. It produces a flat seam, and may be used on garments made by beginners who are unable to work sewing and felling.

Prepare thus : Turn down the raw edges of the material with a narrow fold, one piece to the *wrong* side, and the other on to the *right*. Lay the raw edge of one piece over the edge of the other, so that it effectually covers the turnings ; this overlapping should be about as wide as an ordinary seam. Fix the edge in place, and fell it down. Turn to the other side of the material, and fell it similarly.

Fig. 103 shows the seam with one side felled and the other in progress.

VI. A Counter-hemmed Seam Machined.—This same kind of seam could be stitched on the right side, one line of stitches securing the fold on the *right* side, and another line (worked on the right side) securing the fold on the wrong.   (Fig. 104.)

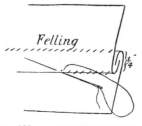
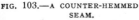
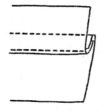

FIG. 103.—A COUNTER-HEMMED   FIG. 104.—A COUNTER-HEMMED
SEAM.   SEAM MACHINED.

VII. A Stitched Seam.—This is the method usually adopted on dress materials, and the one which the sewing machine works so perfectly. The material is, as a rule, lined for this kind of seam. It is used where great strength is needed. The raw edges are placed evenly, with the right sides of material facing. The stitching is worked at a certain distance below the edge, according to the thickness of the material. The raw edges are trimmed of frayings, flattened out right and left, and over-cast. (Sometimes the seams are over-cast at the edges, without previous flattening.)

VIII. Flannel Seams.—Described in Chapter IX.

IX. Machined Seams.—This method is suitable for any material. The material is fixed on the *right* side as for a run-and-fell, stitched on the *right* side where the *right* side of the running would come, and the fell flattened down and stitched again. It is similar in appearance to Fig. 104, and forms an ornamental seam for any garment, if the machining is worked regularly. It is invariably used in shirtmaking, and should be generally adopted on all machine-made garments.

CHAPTER XXI

OVER-CASTING

I. Remarks.—This stitch is used for neatening purposes, to prevent raw edges from fraying. It is not a recognised stitch upon any kind of calico work—belonging chiefly to dress material.

There are two methods usually adopted.

II. Directions for Working. 1st Method.—Commonly used for neatening seams in bodices. Carefully trim the raw edges. Over-casting is worked from left to right. Hold the material along the finger as for sewing, only in readiness to begin at the left-hand side. Run the needle parallel with the edge for $\frac{1}{2}$

FIG. 105.—1ST METHOD.　　　FIG. 106.—2ND METHOD.

an inch, and bring it out about $\frac{1}{8}$ of an inch down. Hold the work so that the thumb and finger cover the raw edge while drawing the needle out for commencement, as the material will be less likely to fray. Insert the needle a short distance to the right and bring it out about $\frac{1}{8}$ in. down. Always draw the cotton out towards the right hand. The stitches should not be too close—eight to an inch are ample. (Fig. 105.) Generally the quicker over-casting is done, the more regular it is likely to be. Fasten off by running the needle parallel with the edge.

2nd Method.—(Fig. 106.) This is the embroidery stitch (sometimes erroneously called button-hole stitch, but it will be noticed that a twist of the cotton is at the edge, whereas the button-hole edge has a knot). It is also used for the purpose of neatening blankets, hence it is often called " blanket stitch." The wrong

side of a print patch is worked in this way, as is also the
scalloped edge on any flannel garment.

Hold the material so that the raw edge faces the worker, and
the bulk of the article lies over the hand. Begin at the left-
hand corner, running the needle down at right angles to the raw
edge. Hold the cotton under the thumb. Insert the needle a
short distance to the right ; the depth that the over-casting is
needed will regulate how much material is to be taken on needle,
but do not loose the thumb till cotton is almost home. The
distance the stitches are apart will depend upon the article in
hand, 8 or 10 to an inch are usually sufficient. Each stitch is
made in the same way. Be careful not to pull the cotton too
tightly, or the raw edge will turn under and make a ridge. To
fasten off, run the cotton in the direction of the stitch, *i.e.*, at
right angles to the edge, and secure it by a backstitch before
cutting the thread.

CHAPTER XXII

CUTTING MATERIAL ON THE CROSS—A FALSE HEM— A PIPING CORD

I. Introduction.—Material cut on the cross (*i.e.*, at an angle of 45°) is used for the purpose of neatening raw edges which are curved, such as necks and armholes of garments, and which, if hemmed without the addition of the crossway piece or " false hem " as it is termed, would not set well.

The advantage of using material on the cross lies in its power to give or stretch, and in dressmaking and millinery also it serves a most useful purpose.

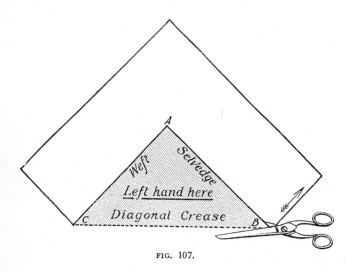

FIG. 107.

II. Preparation of the Material.—Crossway cutting is rather wasteful if long pieces are required, so that joins are often made in the strips for the sake of economy. It is the simplest plan to cut from material in which one corner is a right angle.

Lay the material right side downwards. Fold over one of the corners, so that the crease made is the diagonal of a square, which means that *A* (Fig. 107) must be on the same *line of thread* as *B* and *C*. Any other angle will not give the " true cross of the material."

109

Place the diagonal fold to the worker, and put the left hand flat upon the material. Insert the scissors as shown and through the fold, being careful to stretch the fold to its fullest extent while cutting. Both the cut edges will be on the cross, and the strips can be cut from either piece according to the length required.

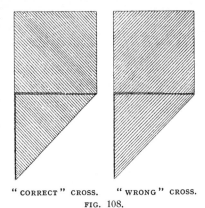

" CORRECT " CROSS.   " WRONG " CROSS.

FIG. 108.

Determine the width of the strip, and measure along the *straight edges* 1½ *times the depth* required, and put *small* snips. Fold the material over, and crease the depth of the strip *exactly even* (pinning if necessary), and cut in the crease. Other strips can be cut by placing the *first* one on the cross edge as a guide.

Measuring 1½ times *on the selvedge* for the amount required for the depth *on the cross* will give a measure *slightly in excess* of the amount, *e.g.*, if a crossway strip 3 in. in depth is needed, and 4½ in. be measured on the straight and then folded, the depth through the strip will be slightly more than 3 in.—about 3⅙ in.—but the even calculation is sufficiently accurate for all practical work.

If the fabric be twilled, or has a " grain," such as merino, serge, cashmere, plush, crape, etc., be careful to fold the corner over, so that the little lines of the twill look perpendicular to the fold, as the appearance is not effective if the lines run across. (Fig. 108.)

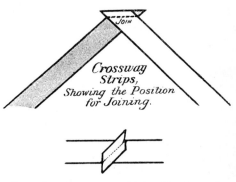

Crossway Strips, Showing the Position for Joining.

Showing Crossway Join flattened out. The Projecting Points to be Cut off to make the Strips even.

FIG. 109.

If the strips cut are not of sufficient length, they must be joined. Place the *right* sides of the strips touching, and cross the ends so that the strips form a **Λ**, by placing the sharp-pointed end to the blunt-pointed end, and leaving the sharp ends projecting about ⅙ in. beyond the sides; otherwise, when joined and flattened the two pieces will not be even along the slanting edge. Run the edges ⅙ in. down and flatten out the seam right and left. Cut off the projecting points at each side. (Fig. 109.) The join will be scarcely noticeable when finished. In garment-making strips have often to be cut from irregularly-shaped material, but the folding must always be at 45° and the ends cut *exactly* by a thread before being joined.

A FALSE HEM.

I. Use.—False hems are often used round the armholes, necks, and fronts of garments. They are most suitable for curved edges, and have the advantage of not depriving the garment of any width except the turning.

False hems may be on " the straight " or " the cross." The method of working is the same, only the latter requires more skill,

II. Directions for Fixing—

1. Place the *right* side of the strip to the *right* side of the garment—edge to edge.

2. Run evenly close to the raw edges, and break open the join.

3. Fold over the strip to the wrong side, making the join come *exactly* at the edge.

4. Turn under the raw edge carefully for ⅙ in., slightly stretching crossway material if required to make it set flatly and fell the strip to the garment.

If the false hem is required to come to the edge of a placket, the strip must be cut off, leaving ¼ in. for turning, and the edges must be turned in and the corner sewn up.

A PIPING CORD.

I. Use.—This is another method of finishing off the neck and armholes of garments, or any curved edge. Cotton cord, some-times called " bobbin," can be bought in various sizes, and is enclosed in a crossway piece of material. The strip should be cut 1¼ in. wide.

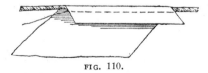

FIG. 110.

II. Directions for Working.—To Put in the Cord : Hold the crossway strip the wrong side uppermost, placing the cord a good ¼ in. from the top edge. Fold this edge over the cord, and tack in place close under the roll. (Fig. 110.)

To Attach the Cording to the Material.—The *sides* of the garment must be hemmed, or at least tacked, before the piping is applied. Place the piping with its raw edge facing downwards on to the right side of garment, about ¼ in. from the

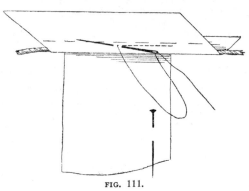

FIG. 111.

edge of the material. Be sure a good margin is left at the right hand, so that the top corner of the crossway material is at least ¼ in. from the edge of the garment. Stitch or run-stitch in place close up to the cording, taking the stitches well through. (Fig. 111.) When the stitching is complete, turn the work to the wrong side and flatten down the crossway piece so that the corded edge shows clearly on the right side. The corner should now be cut straight, allowing for turnings, and the *cord cut close to the edge of the garment* before turning under the edges, or clumsiness will result. A narrow fold must be made along the crossway edge and felled down to the garment, and the other corner neatened in the same way as the commencement.

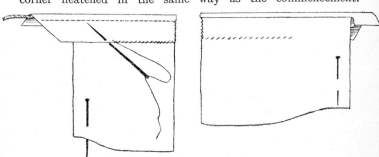

FIG. 112.—WRONG SIDE.　　　　FIG. 113.—RIGHT SIDE.

Note.—The *edge* of the side of the garment to which the piping is attached would always be hemmed first—these hems are not shown in the small illustrations.

(Figs. 112 and 113.) If the material be lined, it is not necessary to let the stitches show through. The crossway edge may be stretched to make it set well, if it is to be felled round a curve.

CHAPTER XXIII

EYELET-HOLES, LOOPS, HOOKS, EYES

I. Description.—Eyelet-holes, loops, and eyes are means used, in conjunction with a hook, to fasten different parts of a garment together, which need to be close fitting.

On garments which are bought ready made these details are invariably poor, and it is nearly always necessary to set on buttons, work eyelets in the proper places, and secure hooks and loops before a garment is worn.

Eyelet-holes are also used as an outlet for a draw string at the waist or neck of a garment. Hooks and eyes are not often used in underclothing, and if put upon washing materials intended for ironing only, a stain is frequently left in the fabric ; buttons and button-holes, or loops, are preferable in any case.

When small pearl or linen buttons are used, and particularly on parts of garments where trimming is arranged, there is often a difficulty in finding a suitable place for a button-hole, and the loop is then the best means of fastening.

II. Directions for Working—Eyelets.—These are worked on *single* or *double* material according as needed for an outlet for a tape or to receive a hook. The hole should always be pierced with a stiletto (which is a pointed steel implement with a round, smooth shank, gradually increasing in size from point to hilt), and the piercing made sufficiently large to enable the tape to pass in easily when threaded through the bodkin. In ready-made garments the tape is frequently run through the neck or waist and brought out *at the ends* of the band, which makes it impossible to fasten the garment so that it wraps over and is neat when the tape is secured.

On the necks and waists of children's garments which are intended to draw up to fit more closely, the position of the eyelet must be determined by the amount the garment overlaps, *e.g.*, if a band wraps for *one* inch, the eyelets must be put half an inch in from each end of the band, thus : At the *under* or *right*-hand side of the band, and on the *upper* or *left*-hand side ; a wrap of ¾ in. would need eyelets ⅜ in. from the edge, and a similar division for other arrangements. When tape is inserted in this manner it can be tied, and the bow and ends are quite easily hidden under the fastenings. It is always advisable to have the tape sufficiently long to allow the band to flatten out for laundry purposes, and it should be stitched in the middle to prevent it from being withdrawn. Very narrow *linen* tape should always be used or else French braid, which is best suited to fine cambrics or muslins.

There are three methods of working.

1st Method.—(Fig. 114.) Slip the needle between the folds, and bring it out at the edge of the hole and in such a position

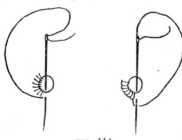

that the inset of the tape is not impeded—grip the material very firmly between the thumb and left forefinger, and *tightly* overcast the edge of hole all round from left to right, gradually turning the material round as work proceeds—pass the needle to the wrong side, make a back-stitch, slip it between the fold and cut the cotton. The edge of the hole should feel like a piece of fine twine.

FIG. 114.

1ST METHOD.   2ND METHOD.

2nd Method.—(Fig. 114.) Slip the needle between the fold and bring it out about ⅛ in. from the raw edges of the hole—hold the cotton under the thumb—put the needle into the hole and bring it out slightly to the right of the cotton—loose the thumb and draw the cotton tightly towards the worker.

Continue working in this way all round the hole and fasten off as described above.

Fig. 118 shows a band (miniature in length), and illustrates—

1. The half and quarter marks.

2. The position of the eyelet-holes when a band is intended to wrap over for 1 in.

3. The tape inserted.

3rd Method.—A *long* eyelet-hole (really a button-hole on *single* material) is frequently used on a waist-band as an outlet for a drawstring. It is worked similarly to a button-hole, and the tape inserted into the case formed by two lines of stitching.

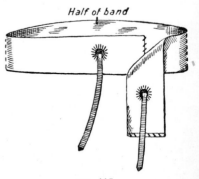

Half of band

FIG. 115.

Loop.—(Fig. 116.) This consists of several strands of cotton, passed over and through the material to form a foundation upon which to work over-casting, in order to make a firm edging for the hook or button. The twist of the over-casting stitch forms the outside portion of the loop, so that the hook rests on the rounded edge. A loop should be made on the under side of a band or trimming, and at a sufficient distance from the end to allow the garment to wrap over, when buttoned, as much as is allowed for in the arrangement of the opening.

To Form the Strands.—Slip the needle between the folds, and bring it out at the right side. Put the needle in a short distance to the right (a good ¼ in. for a hook, ¾ in. for a loop), and bring it out again at the starting-place. Repeat this process till three or four strands are formed (fine cotton would need more foundation threads). Be careful to keep the strands an even length. If the loop be needed to pass over a button, as is sometimes the case for small articles, such as babies' frocks or pinafores, the strands should be left *sufficiently slack* to allow the button to pass through *easily* (there is always a tendency to make a loop for a button too small).

FIG. 116. FIG. 117.

To Work the Edging.—A loop for a button should be pinned down as in Fig. 117, in order to make the strands firm for working the edge.

Commence from the left hand, hold the cotton down with the left thumb, put the needle under the strand (the eye of needle is preferable), and draw it out towards the chest, loosing the thumb hold as the cotton is drawn home. Repeat till the strands are covered. To fasten off, pass the needle to the wrong side, make a backstitch, slip between the fold, and cut the thread.

The beauty of the loop consists in the uniformity with which the stitches are made. The quicker the working the more regular the appearance, as a rule.

Hooks and Eyes.—(Fig. 118.) Strength and neatness are the two features to consider.

The best way to secure these fastenings to a garment is to over-cast or button-hole the rings of wire on to the material,

FIG. 118.

and to fasten the hook by strands of thread crossing the shank. The eye should be over-cast all round so that no part of the metal shows. Fasten off by backstitches as for a loop. Occasionally it is necessary to fasten a hook to a garment with the shank uppermost ; in this case, the hook would only be secured by the rings of wire. Hooks are sometimes sewn on in this manner for a loose-fitting garment, because the hook is more likely to remain fastened if this method be adopted.

CHAPTER XXIV

GATHERING AND SETTING ON A SKIRT TO A BODICE

I. Introduction.—The skirts of children's frocks and petticoats are attached to a band in rather a different manner from the ordinary method of setting in gathers.

II. Preparation of Material.—After the placket slit is formed, the upper part of the skirt should be divided into half, quarters, and eighths, and each of these divisions marked with cotton a few inches below the edge. The raw edge should be neatly over-cast. (*See* Chap. XXI.)

If a thin material this edge might be hemmed, but it will add to the bulkiness of the waist, or it is a quick method to fold it once very narrowly and run it.

Turn down a fold about ½ in. in depth on to the wrong side. Take a good length of cotton, stouter than that in ordinary use on the garment; but if fine muslin or cambric it would be as well to use fine cotton double, so that it will not require a coarser needle, which would be likely to make holes in the material. Gather *close* to the edge of the fold on the right side, passing over *double* the quantity of material taken on the needle, being careful that the needle goes *through* the fold every time. Do not begin with a knot—a few backstitches are preferable.

If the material of the skirt is considerably more than double the length of the band on the bodice, the gathers may be made a little larger accordingly, so that each division of the skirt may be set on to its corresponding piece of band, regularly and without excessive fullness.

Unthread the needle at each quarter and take fresh cotton—begin again just in front of the old end. When the gathering is complete, the work will require stroking carefully. (*See* Chap. XI.)

The skirt is now ready to be put on the bottom of the bodice.

III. Attaching the Skirt to the Bodice.—Place the right side of the skirt to the right side of the bodice—edge to edge. Loosen the gathers, and pin half, quarters, and eighths of the bodice to the same divisions of the skirt.

Carefully adjust the gathering cotton round the pins, and arrange the gathers regularly with the needle. Tack, if preferred. It is usual to hold the fullness towards the worker, but

116

some people find it more convenient to keep the band to the worker, because the gathering thread is then at the left hand, and so is ready for readjustment, if necessary.

Fig. 119 shows the end flattened out, so that the setting-on stitch can be easily seen. For practical work, both gathers and band are held between the thumb and forefinger. The edge of each gather is attached to the band by what may be called a " double sewing stitch." The sewing stitch is worked in the usual way, and then another stitch is taken, bringing the needle out, without advancing any distance, in the same place as the cotton comes from. The stitch appears in the shape of the letter N.

If the gathers are very close this double stitch need not be taken at *every* gather. Care is necessary when passing the halves and quarters to make the division as invisible as possible.

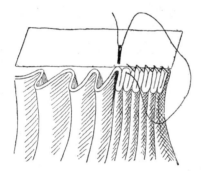

FIG. 119.—SETTING GATHERS OF A FROCK ON TO A BODICE.

Thread the needle with the gathering cotton when the work is complete, and fasten it off neatly on the wrong side. Flatten out the gathers from the band.

Sometimes a double row of gathering is worked, which has the effect of making the gathers more regular. The second row must be parallel with the first and exactly the same proportions kept.

IV. Remarks.—A more fanciful way of working is to put the skirt on so that a frill is seen on the right side just under the waist. Decide upon the depth of frill, and turn down a fold on to the wrong side the required depth of the frill, adding $\frac{1}{2}$ in. for turning on the wrong side.

Now turn the folded edge over on the *right* side for the depth of frill, and gather through the four thicknesses close to the edge. Set on to the band in the usual way, when the frill will be hanging loose on the right side.

This method is only suitable for thin material.

Another plan is to gather the skirt on the single stuff, a good $\frac{1}{4}$ in. from the edge. The band on the bodice must in this case be split in half, set on in the ordinary way, as for single material, and the other half of the band used to neaten the raw edges on the wrong side.

Yet another way of arranging is as follows : Turn down a narrow hem ($\frac{1}{8}$ in.) on the wrong side of garment, and keep the wrong side facing worker. Secure the cotton at the fold of the skirt by a backstitch. Take a stitch as for ordinary gathering at the lower part of the hem. At a short distance to the right of last stitch, take a similar stitch at the fold of skirt, which will show strands of cotton reaching from the top to the bottom of the hem. Continue working alternately at the edges of the fold, which, when drawn up, will show a quantity of little rucks, quite neat on the wrong side, and forming an effective sloping appearance on the right. Set the skirt on to the band as shown in Fig. 119.

CHAPTER XXV

SCALLOPING

I. Remarks.—Scalloping is a term used in needlework, to signify the working and cutting out of a border to resemble the edge of a scallop's shell.

A strict plain needlewoman may perhaps regard this as a branch of fancy work, but, as its adoption forms a pleasing variety to an otherwise plain garment, a description of the mode of working may not be out of place.

II. Uses.—To ornament the edge of any garment, such as a petticoat, barracoat or baby's long flannel, head flannel, bodice, cami-knickers, etc.

III. Preparation of Material.—At the bottom of a petticoat, scalloping should be worked on double material; therefore it is necessary to make a deep hem, say, $2\frac{1}{2}$ to 3 in., as the sloping of the scallops will tend to narrow it. Transfer patterns can be obtained with scallops of various sizes, stamped upon tissue paper, in readiness to transfer to the material. This paper can be bought from any draper selling fancy goods. Its cost is trifling, varying according to size and pattern.

To Transfer the Pattern.—Lay a clean cloth over the edge of the flannel, and pass a warm iron over the cloth in order to smooth the nap or fluff of the flannel. The iron should be tested with the paper before using it on the garment. Lay the transfer paper, right side downwards, just to the edge of the hem—pass a moderately hot iron over the paper, drawing it up from the flannel with the left hand as the iron is removed (if the paper is allowed to remain on the material it is apt to stick). A second person would be an assistance to guide the transfer paper at the edge of the material, just in advance of the iron. Scalloping may be worked upon flannel with either wool or silk. A coarse crewel needle is suitable.

The beauty of the work consists in the regularity of the scallops, the even tension of each stitch, and the absence of puckering.

In order to give the full raised effect to the stitches, it is necessary to lay a padding of wool or knitting cotton close to the outline—this is suitable even if silk be used for scalloping, as this thickening is hidden by the working. The diagram illustrates the manner of placing the padding, which consists of a strand of wool or knitting cotton run from one corner to the other *just below* the point of the scallop, and left sufficiently loose to fit round the outline of the pattern. A very narrow scallop would not need any padding.

119

IV. Method of Working the Stitch.—(Fig. 120.)

1. Hold the edge of the garment to the worker.

2. Work from left to right.

3. Slip the needle between the folds and bring it out at the outer edge of the scallop.

4. Hold the thread under the left thumb, making a loop from left to right.

5. Insert the needle just outside the *inner* outline of the scallop, and bring it out again to the right of the thread, loose the thumb and draw gently towards the worker. This produces a twist at the edge.

6. Continue working thus, letting the stitches just touch each other, so as to hide the padding effectually, adapting

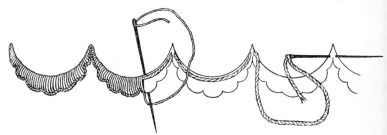

COMPLETED   SCALLOP IN PROCESS   SCALLOP   OUTLINE OF
SCALLOP.   OF WORKING.   PADDED.   SCALLOP SHOWING
                                      STRANDING.

FIG. 120.

the length of each stitch to the shape and size of each scallop. Care is necessary at the corners, to make the stitches taper nicely and set well. All joins are effected by slipping the needle between the folds of the material, the new thread being brought out just in the twist where the old stitch ended. This process is often erroneously called " button-hole stitch," and the edge spoken of as a " button-hole edge." It is known as such to workers of embroidery, and is apt to mislead a worker of plain needlework ; but by reference to the chapter on button-holing, it will be seen that the method of holding, manner of working, and appearance of the edge, are quite different from the button-hole stitch of *plain* needlework.

The method of working a scalloped edge is similar in principle to that adopted for over-casting a print patch.

V. Shaping the Edge.—After the working is complete, the edge is shaped. A pair of small, sharp scissors are necessary. Hold the garment right side uppermost, with the scallops to the right hand, and cut the material away. Be *very careful* not to cut the threads of the working. The cutting is rather a slow process, and is best done a little at a time, as the general finish of the work can be so soon spoiled by hurried cutting.

CHAPTER XXVI

HEM-STITCHING

I. Introduction.—This may be considered a branch of fancy work, but as the process is sometimes adopted on children's frocks, aprons, pocket-handkerchiefs, sheets, and other articles of house linen, it may almost be recognised as plain needle-work. The sampler of olden times, spoken of in the Chapter on " Marking," invariably had a hem-stitched border. The hem-stitch is also used to prevent fringes at the ends of towels from further ravelling, and so becoming untidy.

Hem-stitching is principally used in the lately revived " drawn thread embroidery," where most effective, inexpensive and exceedingly pretty specimens of work can be done, if one has the patience, ambition, industry, good eyesight, finger skill, and the amount of leisure time which the work necessarily involves.

II. Definition.—Hem-stitching, as its name suggests, consists of a hem fixed in the ordinary way, *perfectly straight by a thread*, with a certain number of the threads of the material withdrawn just below the hem. These threads are arranged in clusters of three, four, five, or six, and fastened to the fold of the hem by stitching, which produces small, open spaces between each cluster of threads.

III. Material Used.—It is advisable to practise on a coarse fabric, where the threads can be easily seen. Cheese-cloth canvas and Oxford shirting are suitable materials for practice purposes. The principal drapers sell a soft even-threaded linen which is specially suited for drawn thread work. The size of the cotton must be regulated by the coarseness of the threads of the material. For very fine work, lace thread is sometimes used.

IV. Preparation of Material.—Decide on the width of hem, according to the requirement of the article in hand, and fold it down in the ordinary way. The hem may be either on the right or wrong side according to the material ; it must be quite even, and *strictly by a thread*, or the general appearance will be spoiled. *Just below* the fold draw out as many threads as are necessary, which will depend upon the texture of the material and the required size of the interspaces. On *coarse* material two or three threads are generally sufficient. After the first thread is withdrawn the others are easily removed. Fix the hem so that the folded edge is exactly level with the *upper* part of the drawn threads.

V. Method of Working.—There are several methods of hem-stitching, each worked in a slightly different way, and, although the shape of the stitches may not be alike in each method, the result, viz., the open work, is practically the same. The simplest method is described here, and is worked from *left*

121

to right, as the work is held, although in the illustrations which *face the worker*, the stitch appears from *right to left*. Hold the work over the fingers of the left hand, *so that the folded edge of the hem is towards the worker*, and somewhat in the same position as if setting in gathers. If the work be held as for ordinary hemming, the stitches cannot be kept close up to the folded hem, and this is an essential feature of the work.

1. Commence as for ordinary hemming, when the cotton will be upon the fold of the hem.

*2. Put the needle in just underneath where the cotton is brought out, and in the drawn threads, taking up horizontally upon the needle a certain number of strands (three in illustration). Any number may be taken up, varying with the size of the threads of the material. (Fig. 121.)

 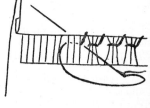

FIG. 121. FIG. 122.

3. Insert the needle back in the same place as for ordinary stitching, and bring it out in the usual manner for simple hemming, just on the edge of the fold, and exactly above the end of the backstitch. (Fig. 122.)

4. Repeat from * till the hem is secured throughout its length.

If the stitch be analysed it will be seen to consist of three parts—

(*1*) The stitch taking up the required number of threads *as for running*.

(*2*) The needle being put back *as for stitching*.

(*3*) The needle taking up the threads *as for hemming*, which has the effect of drawing the threads in groups, and at the same time securing the fold of the hem, with the needle in readiness for making the next stitch.

The cotton should be drawn rather tightly as each stitch comes home, but not in any way to pucker the material, which must lie perfectly flat, with a regular and even distribution of threads to each stitch.

The join in the cotton is made as for simple hemming.

CHAPTER XXVII

MARKING

I. Introduction.—The art of marking was brought to perfection many years ago, and if our great-grandmothers could but see the meagre attempts made by us, they would have some contempt for the system by which our needlework abilities are tested.

Who does not remember having seen often in a frame the " yellow with age " sampler, showing the alphabet, capital and small, in Latin, Gothic and Old English script ; the figures ; an appropriate text or verse ; sundry ornithological specimens ; a few representations of animals, trees and flowers ; generally a cross and crown, with the name and age of worker, and the date of the year to conclude the achievement : all being surmounted by a handsome border ?

These samplers were considered a certain test of proficiency in needlework and proof of skill, and they were treasured with such care that many worked during the eighteenth century are even now in a good state of preservation.

A sampler, dated 1761, was shown recently at an exhibition. The verse was, to say the least, quaint. It read as follows—

> Hannah White is my name,
> And with my needle I worked the same,
> That all the world may clearly see
> What care my parents took of me.

The utility of all this work, beyond that of cultivating habits of perseverance and neatness, may be questioned, and certainly time and talent may be more profitably employed.

Marking, even in its simplest form, has suffered since the invention of marking ink, which, although an expeditious method, does not look so well as marking with thread, neither is it suitable to every kind of material. Machine embroidered letters can also be bought in almost any combination, but although people consider marking an unnecessary stitch, there are still many households in which linen and underclothing are marked with cotton ; certainly the cost is comparatively *nil*, and the articles are rendered ornamental, tidy, and finished, and have the advantage of being easily discerned by the laundress, or distinguished from clothing belonging to other members of the family.

Students are advised to spend very little time at this work, but it is essential that the formation of the letters should be known so that they may be readily copied.

II. Material used.—Marking should be taught upon Java canvas ; when proficiency is gained, coarse marking linen or Saxony cloth may be used, and finally flannel, calico, and finer linen. Marking cotton can be bought either in skeins or reels, in numbers varying from 40 to 120. It is dyed previous to twisting, hence it is "ingrain." Turkey-red is the common colour. This contrasts well with white material. Blue marking cotton can also be bought. Any colour is suitable for practice.

III. Varieties of Marking—

1. The ordinary cross-stitch, producing a cross on the right side, and an irregular stitch on the wrong. This is the simplest kind of marking.

2. " True " marking, in which both right and wrong sides form a cross.

3. " Eyelet-hole," in which each stitch is worked to its centre.

4. " Queen," or Spanish stitch, consisting of a square on the right side and a cross on the wrong.

5. " Stitching " or " chain-stitching " a pencilled letter.

1. Description of Cross-stitch Marking.—This is generally worked from left to right, and each stitch crosses a square of two threads.

Commencement.—Bring the needle through, between the threads, from the underneath to the right side, leaving a finger length of cotton, which can be darned in when work is finished. On no account use a knot.

The Stitch—

1. Count two threads to the right, and take up two threads perpendicularly, bringing the *point of the needle out on a line with the cotton.* This forms the first diagonal or under portion of the stitch. (Fig. 123.)

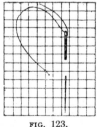

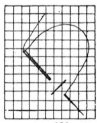

FIG. 123.   FIG. 124.

2. Insert the needle at the top left-hand corner, two threads *above* the starting-point, and bring the needle out at the left-hand corner of the place needed for the next stitch. (Fig. 124.)

The upper portion of the cross has now been made, the thread slanting from *right to left*. Each stitch is worked in the same way.

There are other ways of inserting the needle in order to form the cross-stitch, producing exactly the same result on the right side.

Another method is shown in Figs. 125 and 126.

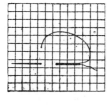   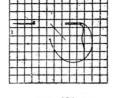

FIG. 125.   FIG. 126.

It is advisable to work a number of stitches to gain familiarity and speed.

Finish.—Fasten off by running the cotton under the last few stitches on the wrong side and cut close. Thread the needle with the end left at the commencement and treat in the same way. This is a point that must be insisted upon in class teaching, otherwise good marking is often spoiled by want of attention to the neatness of the wrong side.

For commencement, the end of cotton may be worked in with the first few stitches, if preferred. It is rather more difficult for a child to manage, and requires more practice.

Knots in marking are very hideous, and should not be permitted under any circumstances—they are quite unnecessary.

The Alphabet—

1. Capital letters are seven stitches high, consisting of fourteen threads ; usually four or five threads are left between each letter.

2. Every letter must be *complete* by itself. A strand of cotton must *not*, upon any account, be passed from one letter to another, and so make a connection on the wrong side, but each letter should be finished off before the next is commenced.

3. Each stitch should be crossed the same way.

4. Letters on underclothing and house linen are usually marked *weft* way of the material, *i.e.*, the selvedge threads running from top to bottom of the letter.

As soon as the stitch is known, the capital letters of the alphabet may be taught.

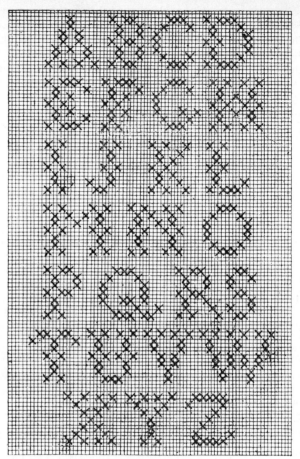

FIG. 127.—THE ALPHABET.

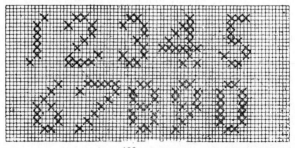

FIG. 128.—FIGURES.

These must be introduced in a step-wise succession of difficulty (not in alphabetical order), thus—

1. The letter " I " is the simplest, and enters into the formation of several other letters.

2. E, F, H, L, T, K, M, and N contain portions of " I."

3. " O " is the easiest of the round letters.

4. C, G, and Q are variations of the circle.

5. B, D, J, P, R, U, are a combination of " I " and " O."

6. A, V, W have the same kind of slope.

7. S, X, Y, and Z are dissimilar, and must be taught separately.

Excellent practice in marking from memory is afforded by studying the construction of a letter, and reproducing it on paper.

Small letters are five threads high, the tall-small letters generally seven ; two threads between each letter are sufficient.

Exactly the same rules as above apply to numerals.

Figs. 127 and 128 give an illustration of the alphabet and figures.

2. " True " Marking.—This stitch was known many years ago as " Brave Bred " stitch. It consists in producing the same appearance on the *wrong* side as the *right*, viz., a cross.

It cannot be called " letter-perfect " on the wrong side, as of course, some letters will appear as though shaped backwards, *e.g.*, C, F, G, K, L, etc.

It requires exceptionally *fine* cotton for the stitch, otherwise it is a shapeless mass.

Description of True Marking.

Bring the needle through to the right side, leaving a finger length of cotton ; put the needle in at the right-hand top corner

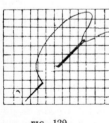 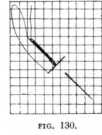 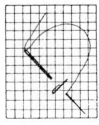

FIG. 129.   FIG. 130.   FIG. 131.

of the square of threads over which the stitch is to be made, and bring the needle out at the bottom left-hand corner, exactly where the cotton starts from—this forms a diagonal stitch on both right and wrong sides. (Fig. 129.) The next stitch consists of a *half* stitch taken only as far as the centre of the diagonal (Fig. 130), and if possible underneath the whole cotton, the needle being brought out at either of the other corners which seem most convenient for the next stitch of the letter that is being formed (a little practice and foresight will soon show the suitable position for the needle) ; make another diagonal stitch as before, which will complete the cross on both the right and wrong sides. (Fig. 131.) It will be seen that portions of the stitch are crossed *twice*, hence the necessity for using fine cotton, and to form some letters it is needful to cross even more than twice, in order to bring the needle out in the place required. The fastening off consists in making a diagonal stitch over one or two stitches already made, and cutting the cotton close ; treat the thread left at the commencement similarly.

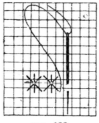

FIG. 132.

3. Eyelet-hole Stitch.—This consists of eight stitches, each of which is worked to its centre.

The diagram sufficiently illustrates the working (Fig. 132). This stitch would only be suitable on coarse fabric.

4. Queen, or Spanish Stitch.—This consists of a square on the right side and a cross on the wrong. It is worked by making a backstitch above, below, and on either side of a square of threads. It is worked from right to left. The needle is put in perpendicularly, diagonally, or horizontally, as required to form the stitch, an illustration of which is given on the canvas sampler at the end of the book.

5. Stitching, or Chain-stitching a Pencilled Letter.—It is advisable to faintly mark a script letter, taking care to make good curves, and stitch over the line of pencilling. Leave an end of cotton at the commencement, and run at the back of the letter when it is finished.

Chain-stitch is worked thus : Bring the needle through to the right side, hold the cotton down under the left thumb ; insert the needle in exactly the same place as the cotton comes out ; take up two threads upon the needle (or a proportionate amount of material), keeping the needle to the *right-hand* side of the cotton ; draw *gently* towards the worker, which will form the first stitch. Hold the cotton under the thumb ; put the needle back in the chain just made, and exactly in the same place as the cotton comes out, and so on. (Fig. 133.) Fasten off as for stitching. The right side will appear as the links in a chain, or similar to the simple stitch in crochet work, being a loop proceeding from a previously formed loop.

A chain-stitch sewing machine produces on the wrong side a *facsimile* of this stitch.

If preferred, a letter may be pencilled on soft paper, tacked on the top of the material, the stitch worked over the pencilling, and then the paper pulled away.

FIG. 133.

IV. Position of Marking on House Linen and Garments.—Bed, house, and table linen, also kitchen towels, are usually marked at the upper left-hand corner thus—

Name	.	.	.	.	A. Jones.
No. of articles	.	.	.		6.
Year	.	.	.	.	1934.

Pocket-handkerchiefs are marked at the same corner.

Underclothing at the lower part of front opening.

Stockings at the upper part of knee, the loops of the web representing threads. The shape of the letter is sometimes Swiss darned.

V. Faults met with are—

1. Inaccurate formation of the stitch and letter.
2. *Untidy commencement and finish—knots.*
3. Letters connected on wrong side.
4. Material puckered, and general appearance untidy.

PART II

PATCHING

INTRODUCTION

Patching is that method by which any worn-out part of a garment can be restored, by means of a fresh piece of material taking the place of the old.

It is a very humble sort of work, but, nevertheless, an important and necessary branch of mending, requiring the exercise of forethought, straightness of vision, skilful handling, and plenty of patience.

Patches are used when thin places and rents are too worn to be repaired by darning. To " patch " well is equally as important as to " make " well, for by skilfully mending any article, its time of service may be lengthened.

Two different sorts of patching may be noticed—

1. Cutting away the worn material and replacing it by another strong piece.

2. Taking away the worn-out part, and placing an entirely new portion in its stead, *e.g.*, a wristband, collar, sleeves, front of a shirt, etc.   This process is often called " renovating." If a patch be needed anywhere near a seam, the seam should be unpicked, the worn material cut away and new supplied, and then the seam closed again.   This is necessary when patching the under arm of a garment.   Worn material near a band should be treated similarly.

Every kind of material will admit of patching, but calico, print, and flannel are the patches in ordinary use.

The first detail for this description of mending is to obtain material which will match the original in colour, quality, and texture.   This material should not be new for practical work, but good sound pieces of the same stuff as the article in hand. To patch old material with new is merely to make an arrangement for another tear around the patch, as the strain in wear is sure to be too great for the old fabric. The secret of good patching lies in the fixing and the careful removal of the worn part, for if this be cleverly managed the work is sure to be successful. The stitches used in mending are comparatively simple, though requiring a nicety of finish and absence of any pucker. The patch presenting least difficulty is in flannel. For teaching purposes new material will be unavoidable.

The Patches described in Chapters XXVIII–XXX are merely Preliminary to the Practical Work suggested in Chapter XXXI.

CHAPTER XXVIII

A FLANNEL PATCH

I. Introduction.—Material with even threads (Yorkshire flannel is the best for this purpose) should be chosen for the preliminary instruction. It is supposed that practice in herringboning has been given by working strips of flannel, and that the methods of commencing, finishing-off, and joining are *quite familiar and easily managed.* (*See* Chap. VII.)

House flannel and thick yarn or wool for working, form excellent apparatus for demonstration. The patch can be tinted to contrast. (All tints are procurable at any general stores.)

II. Garments likely to need Patching—

Vests.—Under arm and sleeve.

Shirts.—The shoulders, under arms, sleeves and elbows.

III. Shape of Patches.—(1) Square ; (2) oblong; (3) three-cornered or triangular. For practice purposes two pieces of material are necessary, one larger than the other. The large piece will be spoken of as representing the " garment " to be mended, and the smaller the " patch " with which to repair the hole.

IV. Directions for Working a Square or Oblong Patch—

1. Have a hole actually cut in the larger piece to represent the veritable hole if patching a real garment, and *cut* the patch very evenly—quite by a thread. (If the material be torn, the frayings must be cut a couple of threads in so as to have a *clean, firm* edge to the patch.)

2. Find the selvedge way of the garment, and either mark with a pin or place parallel with the desk or table.

3. Find the right side of the garment, and lay it face downwards (the woolly or fluffy side is the right, the wrong side shows the threads more clearly).
   The " fluff " or " nap " should run from left to right.

4. Treat the patch in the same way as the garment (Nos. 2 and 3), and pull the material to straighten it, if necessary.

5. Place the patch on the wrong side of the garment, over the hole and worn part, and *perfectly straight by the threads*, as absolute straightness is most essential ; secure by a few pins. (Be careful that the *selvedge threads of the garment and*

patch are parallel, as this is the fundamental principle of all patching.)

6. Press the patch flatly on to the garment with the hand to make the fibres cling together. Fix the patch all round, close to the edge, or else *above* the position of the herring-bone stitches (say 6 or 8 threads), beginning at the selvedge side, and if preferred, *both* selvedges may be fixed first. *The better the fixing, the flatter the patch.* (As herring-bone stitches protect the raw edge, no turnings are necessary.)

7. Herring-bone the edge of the patch on to the *wrong side of the garment,* holding the edge of the patch to the worker. (Be sure the upper stitches are taken through both thicknesses of material, and that the lower part of the stitch comes *just under* the raw edge.)

It is sometimes recommended that the *right* side be worked first—this is not advisable.

Two good reasons are given for working as described—

(*1*) It is more practical, because, supposing the garment to be a cumbersome one, and the patch needed in an awkward part, having fixed it carefully on the *wrong* side, it is not wise to disarrange the garment for the purpose of treating the right side first.

(*2*) The herring-bone stitches showing through on the right side are a surer guide in cutting away the worn part than merely tacking threads would be.

Perhaps the liability to pucker may be greater, but this may be overcome by *very careful fixing* in the first instance, and *pressing down the edge of the patch with the left thumb while working.*

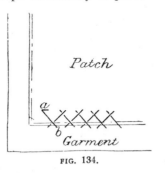

FIG. 134.

Nearly *every* home manager will agree with (1), and the *majority* of teachers with (2).

Should the worker prefer to treat the *right* side first, follow directions Nos. 8 and 9, and come back to 7.

Begin at the *lower left-hand* corner and at the selvedge side ; *a b* in Fig. 134 shows the starting-point. The needle is slipped in on the patch at some distance to the right and brought out at 4 threads *up* on the patch and 4 threads from the left side. The cotton must be secured by a backstitch. Threads must not be counted after commencing, but even distances gauged. The worker should refer to Chapter VII for the method of working the stitch and making a join, and also page 141. Heading V.

The method of turning the outer corner is shown in progress in Fig. 135 and completed in Fig. 136.

To Turn the Corner.—The *last* cross of the *upper* stitch should be at *four* threads (or the depth of the herring-boning) from the adjacent side. If there should be *more* than four threads, the flannel may be cut off evenly along the second side.

Work the lower cross of the stitch.

Insert the needle below the raw edge *on a line with the top of the last cross*, but point it *towards the worker*. (Fig. 135.)

Turn the work round and draw the cotton through.

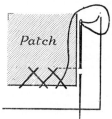

FIG. 135.—SHOWING THE POSITION OF THE NEEDLE IN TURNING THE CORNER.

The inner corner will be formed when the needle is brought *out* to touch the last cross of the upper stitch.

Continue the working.

The fourth side is finished off by making a stitch at the bottom of the first side, crossing in front of the half-stitch, and

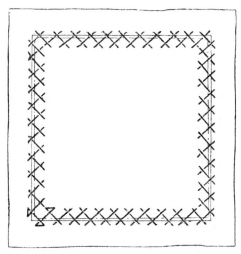

FIG. 136.—PATCH COMPLETE ON WRONG SIDE.

slipping the needle between the folds, and securing by a backstitch on any of the other stitches. (Fig. 136.)

8. Turn the garment to the right side (the herring-bone stitches should show through as two lines of running), and cut away the worn part, leaving *eight threads clear* all round from the *lower* line of the stitches. There should be four threads, or the *depth of the herring-bone stitch*, between the stitches on the right and wrong sides. A good method of cutting away the damaged material is as follows—

1. Put a pin horizontally in the middle of each side, *eight* threads from the *lower line* of the herring-bone stitches.

2. Put the scissors in the hole and cut up to the pins.

3. Remove the pins, and cut parallel with the stitches a piece from each adjacent side alternately, to meet exactly in the corners, so that they form a perfect right angle.

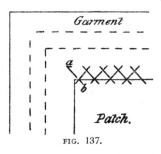

FIG. 137.

Holding the patch to the light will test if all sides are equal. (Excellent practice is given to young pupils by a lesson on a "paper" patch preparatory to the flannel, merely for the purpose of teaching the cutting away of the worn part and acquiring the handling of the scissors. Children sometimes cut away too much, and so spoil the piece of flannel representing the "garment." In the hands of a skilled teacher this is not only a novel but a valuable lesson.)

9. Herring-bone the edge of the garment on to the patch all round the inner square, beginning at the *top* left-hand corner; *a b* in diagram (Fig. 137) shows the starting-point. The needle is slipped in on the garment at some distance to the right, and brought out 4 threads *up* on the garment and 2 threads to the left of the right-angled corner. The cotton is secured by a back stitch. The lower part of the stitch must come *exactly* in the right angle.

The method of turning the inner corner is shown in progress in Fig. 138 and completed in Fig. 139.

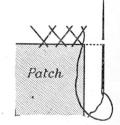

FIG. 138.—SHOWING THE POSITION OF THE NEEDLE IN TURNING THE CORNER.

To Turn the Corner.—Gauge the last few stitches of a side, so that *the lower cross of the last stitch comes exactly in the corner,* even if the stitches have to be put a little closer than the others. Stop at the *upper* part of the last stitch.

Insert the needle 4 threads on the fold and *on a line with the bottom of the last stitch*, but point it *from the worker*. (Fig. 138.)

Turn the work round and draw the cotton through.

The inner corner will be formed when the needle is brought *out* to touch the last cross of the lower part of the stitch.

The stitches, which meet at the corner, form a diamond-shaped or square corner.

The fourth side is finished off from the upper part of the stitch by crossing in front of the half-stitch of the first side,

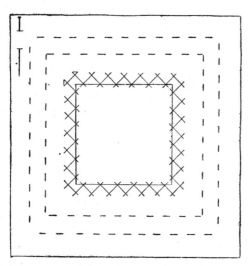

FIG. 139.—PATCH COMPLETE ON RIGHT SIDE.

The lower part of the stitches should meet exactly in each corner.

and slipping the needle between the folds and securing it by a backstitch on any of the other stitches. (Fig. 139.)

V. Faults liable to occur (in addition to those mentioned in connection with herring-boning, p. 46)—

1. Patch and garment not agreeing as regards (*a*) selvedge way of stuff ; (*b*) right and wrong sides ; (*c*) fall of the nap.

2. Patch not fixed to a thread.

3. Corners not correctly turned—*stitches not meeting exactly in each corner.*

4. Patch cut away instead of the worn garment.

5. Too much material cut away, and consequently the fell too narrow.

6. Uneven and puckered in appearance.

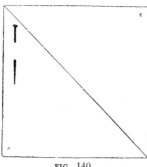

FIG. 140.

TRIANGULAR FLANNEL PATCH.

I. Introduction.—This patch is sometimes used under the arm of a garment, where more often than not the slanting side is joined into a seam. It is also put at the elbows of shirts.

II. Shape of Patch.—This is usually taken from a *square* of flannel, therefore two sides of the patch are cut by the threads of the material and one is on the cross. (Fig. 140.)

III. Directions for Working.—Make a *very* small hole in the centre of the material representing the garment, otherwise it may come in the way when cutting out the worn part. *Exactly*

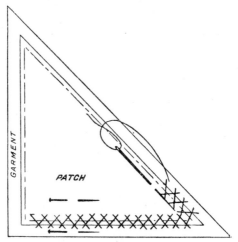

FIG. 141.—SHOWING CORNER ON THE WRONG SIDE.

the same method can be adopted as is used for a square patch, page 135. 1 to 7. Be careful to fix the *selvedge* side first, then the *weft* side (both exactly to a thread), and lastly the *cross* side, which cannot conveniently be stretched if fixed as directed. Begin to work at the right-angled corner, and on the bias side make the stitches match those on the straight side. Great care is necessary in cutting away the worn part on the right side,

---

141

especially along the side which is on the bias. Allow material for the fell of the patch, so that the *depth* of the herring-bone stitch is left *between* the stitches on the right and wrong sides. A line of tacking, or a piece of paper placed parallel with the stitches, would serve as a guide by which to regulate the cutting.

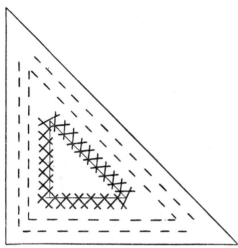

FIG. 142.—PATCH COMPLETE ON THE RIGHT SIDE.

Hold the patch to the light to test its regularity. The diagram gives an idea of the method of turning the corners. (Fig. 141.)

Fig. 142 shows the patch complete.

IV. Faults as in a Square Patch.

V. Remarks.—Many workers commence herring-boning in the middle of one side of the patch—the finish is, in consequence, most conspicuous. In practical repairing the work is naturally commenced at a corner.

Stocking-web material, such as is used for vests, bodices, etc., is frequently patched in the same way as flannel, and produces a good, sound repair.

CHAPTER XXIX

CALICO OR LINEN PATCH

I. Introduction.—The above patch is used to repair weak places and holes in garments and house linen, by the insertion of another piece of material similar to the original.

II. Material Used.—For teaching purposes, new material is generally adopted, because of the difficulty of obtaining worn calico in sufficient quantities, but for "practical mending," new material should not be put upon old fabrics ; good pieces of the same stuff as the article is made of are preferable, or matching it in texture as nearly as possible. If new material must be resorted to, it should be washed before being used, which will remove any "dress," and so the patch will be less likely to make a strain on the worn article.

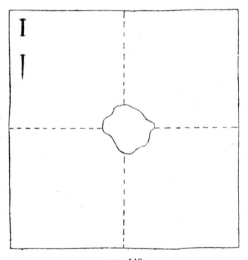

FIG. 143.

III. Directions for Mending.—Calico patching requires great care and skill in fixing, in order that the work may be quite flat and neat when finished. The stitches used for mending are either sewing and felling, or running and felling, so that the difficulty lies in the placing. For practice purposes, two pieces of material are necessary, the larger piece representing the

142

" garment," and the smaller the " patch." The patch must be
sufficiently large to well cover the hole and the worn thin part
which usually surrounds it. The *shape* of the patch, either
square or oblong, can be determined by the hole it is to cover.
Be sure it is cut or torn by a thread, pulled diagonally, and also
selvedge way, to make it perfectly straight.

1. Have a hole actually cut in the larger piece to represent
the true hole if patching a worn article. It is best to fold
the material into four and cut off the folded corner.

2. Fold two creases, one selvedge way and the other weft
way, *i.e.*, at right angles to each other, as nearly as possible
over the centre of the worn part of the garment and quite
evenly by a thread. (Fig. 143.) The material should be
pulled and straightened as directed above.

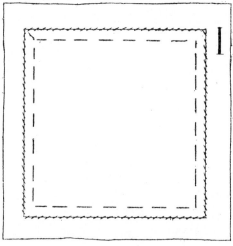

FIG. 144.—WRONG SIDE SHOWING FELLING.

Treat the patch similarly, dividing it by creases into four
equal portions. It is most essential that these folds are all
even with the threads of the fabric.

3. Mark the right side and the selvedge way of the garment
and the patch with a pin. The smooth or glossy side of
calico is the right, the wrong side is rougher looking. This
difference is not noticeable in all cotton materials.

4. Face the *right* side of the garment downwards, with the
selvedge way running even with the desk or table.

5. Turn down a narrow fold ⅛ in. on to the right side of
the patch and even with a thread—selvedge sides first, which

must be *well* stretched, and the weft edges pleated between the fingers to prevent them stretching. The corners should be well pressed—they *must* be at a right angle.

6. Place the patch, with the raw edges downwards, upon the *wrong* side of the garment. *Be very careful that the selvedge threads of both patch and garment run in the same direction* (this is very essential), and that the creases lie exactly on each other. Put in a few small pins.

7. Fix the patch carefully all round, close to the edge and beginning with one of the selvedge sides, keeping the corners

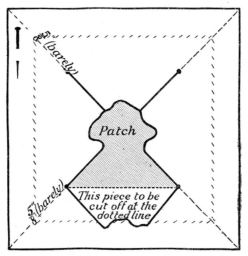

FIG. 145.—RIGHT SIDE SHOWING PREPARATION FOR CUTTING AWAY THE WORN PART.

true to a right angle, and the entire patch, particularly at the selvedge sides, true to a thread. The firmer the fixing, the flatter the patch.

8. *Fell* all round on the *wrong* side before the right is touched, beginning at a corner, as the join will be less conspicuous when the fourth side is worked, and the stitches can be made quite secure. (Fig. 144.) The word "fell" is italicised because many workers get thus far correctly, and then *sew* the patch to the garment, thereby making too great a strain on the already weak material and preparing for another tear.

The worker must read here the reasons stated in favour of this way of working as given under "flannel patching" [page 139, *1* and *2*], reading the word "felling" for "herring-boning."

9. Turn to the right side, and cut away the worn and damaged part by the following method—

1. Make a short diagonal crease from each corner by letting the adjacent sides of the felling touch ; but if the patch is square, the diagonal can be taken from corner to corner.

2. Put a pin prick rather more than ½ an inch (barely ⅝) down the diagonal crease. It is well to measure this distance till the eye is trained to gauge accurately. These pin marks should be *exact* and on the same line of threads. (Fig. 145.)

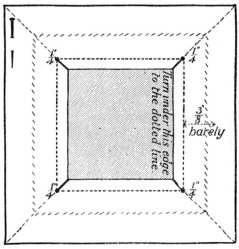

FIG. 146.—RIGHT SIDE SHOWING WORN MATERIAL CUT AWAY.

3. Put the scissors into the hole ; cut up the diagonals as far as the pin-pricks, *and not a trifle beyond.* Use only the *points* of the scissors when cutting close to the pin marks.

4. Fold back each little triangle (with a broken apex), crease the folds, and cut in the creases thus made. (Fig. 145.) Hold up to the light to test if the cutting is regular. Should one of the sides be deeper than the others, make a small snip in the corners, fold back and cut again.

5. Put pin marks ¼ in. *up* the diagonal. Mitre the corners, *i.e.,* snip up at an angle of 45°, as far as pin holes, and not a fraction of an inch beyond. (Fig. 146.)

10. Turn under the raw edge and fix close to the fold, keeping *the corners exactly to a right angle.* The needle can assist in the turning.

Sew all round the inner square, *holding the patch towards the worker* (or the left thumb on the patch is an equivalent), and commencing at a corner as the join will be less conspicuous. If the *garment* be held to the worker, the appearance is somewhat spoiled, as the patch will sink in a shallow instead of being on a level with the surrounding material. Be sure that the needle is put in quite straight in sewing, and that the work is held as described in Chapter IV, otherwise the patch will be puckered.

When the corners are reached, the work should be laid flat and a stitch put in each corner.

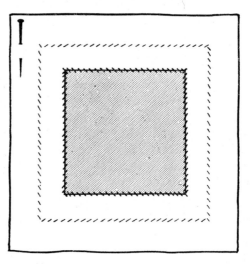

FIG. 147.—PATCH COMPLETE ON THE RIGHT SIDE.

11. Flatten the sewing thoroughly. The fell of the patch should be barely ⅜ of an inch when complete; if much narrower than this the turnings will prevent the patch from being quite flat, especially at the corners. Fig. 147 shows the patch complete. It will be noticed that the *stronger* stitch, viz., sewing, is borne by the *patch*, and the *less strong*, viz., felling, by the thin *garment*, or the *sewing* is at the *inner* or *smaller* square, and the *felling* at the *outer* or *larger* square.

There are other methods of preparing calico patches, and a successful seamstress should be able to adopt any method, and yet produce a good patch; but for school use, it is a question of which plan is easiest for a child to manage. The above method has been most successful, hence the reason for preferring it to other ways of working. If calico or linen to be patched is very thin, and not likely to bear the strain of sewing, the patch may be felled on both the right and wrong sides.

Another common method of working is as follows—

1. Prepare as stated in Nos. 1, 2, and 3 of previous plan.

4. Face the *right* side of garment uppermost.

5. Turn down the patch as for a sew-and-fell seam, nearly ⅜ in. in depth—opposite sides first—press the corners well.

6. Place the patch on the *right* side over the hole, so that selvedge threads of both the patch and the garment are parallel. Fix close to the edge.

7. Sew the edges of the patch to the garment on the right side, being very careful at the corners to avoid catching up the material that forms the fell, otherwise the corners will not flatten out.

8. Turn to the wrong side, and cut away the worn part to within ⅛ in. of the sewing stitches. Make a snip at the corners of the garment.

9. Flatten the sewing, turn down the fell of the patch, and fell it to the garment.

The difficulty with the corners is probably the reason this method is not more popular. Another way, similar to the last, is worked as follows—

Prepare as mentioned in the last method, but instead of turning down as for a sew-and-fell, make *one deep turn*, nearly ⅜ in., on the wrong side of the patch—bend back each corner of the turn, so that it quite frees the folded edge, which will prevent it being caught in with the sewing stitches. Sew the patch to the garment—prepare the wrong side exactly as described in the last method, only the raw edge of the fell will require to be turned under ⅛ in.

This is a successful plan, and deserves to be more widely known.

Another method is to run and fell the patch to the garment. Prepare thus—

Cut away all the worn part of the garment, quite even to a thread—snip the corners slightly—cut the patch quite ½ in. larger than the hole. Place the right sides of the patch and the garment together (selvedges of both running parallel); prepare work as for a run-and-fell (p. 79). Hold the garment to the worker. The running should be about ¼ in. down from the raw edge of the garment. The corners need firm stitches, and the running must be true to a right angle at each corner. Flatten down the fell, and then fell the patch on to the garment.

This is a quick method of patching, but some practice is necessary in order to obtain a nice flat patch.

IV. Faults liable to occur—

1. Selvedge of the patch and the garment not running parallel with each other.

2. Patch unevenly turned and badly fixed—*not straight with the threads of the garment.*

3. The patch *sewn* to the garment on the *wrong* side, instead of being felled.

4. Patch puckered, corners not true to a right angle, badly mitred, and altogether bulky and clumsy.

5. Patch cut away instead of the worn material.

6. Width of patch too narrow or needlessly wide, and turnings not sufficient to be secure.

7. Errors in formation of the stitches used, and also *in the joins*, as described in those chapters.

N.B.—The sewing and felling stitches must match in point of size.

V. Remarks.—A slip of paper, with $\frac{1}{4}$ in. and barely $\frac{3}{8}$ in., marked at the edge, is a very helpful guide to assist the measuring. This can be dispensed with when proficiency is gained. Any plan which helps to secure accuracy of cutting —as this is the difficulty—should be adopted.

CHAPTER XXX

A PRINT OR DRESS PATCH

I. Introduction.—Print is a common make of calico of a loose texture, upon which a coloured pattern is stamped. If this pattern retains its colour in washing, the print is said to be " fast."

Dresses, aprons, children's frocks, and pinafores are the garments usually made of print, and may be worn—or, which is more likely—torn. In such cases, it is necessary to consider the most expeditious way of repairing the damaged material. A print patch is thought to be the least useful of any kind of patch, but the way in which the damaged part is mended may often with advantage be applied to stuff materials, such as serge, beige, tweeds, etc. ; and if silk be used exactly matching the material, and the patch pressed under a damp cloth, it will be almost invisible—this applies to dress stuffs only and not print.

II. Material Used.—For practice purposes new material will probably be needed. There is often a difficulty in obtaining *soft* print, and printed cambrics are used instead, which are more expensive. A *small* pattern repeating itself at short intervals should be selected, and one which requires a little care in matching. (Stripes alone are not sufficient, as they do not give enough scope in matching and present peculiar difficulties themselves.) Print used for practical mending should be washed till it is the same shade as the garment.

Any fabric with a patterned surface can be patched in the same way as print.

III. Directions for Working.—Two pieces of material are necessary, representing " garment " and " patch." It is well to have the patch a good bit larger than the hole, especially if the pattern be difficult to match.

1. Have a *small* hole to mend (if cut too large, it may lead to inconvenience in matching the pattern).

2. Keep the garment right side uppermost.

3. Mark with a pin the selvedge way of the patch and the garment—the stripe or pattern easily shows this.

4. Turn down a fold barely $\frac{3}{8}$ in. upon the wrong side of the patch and on the selvedge sides.

5. Place the patch on the right side of the garment over the hole, *exactly* matching the flower, leaf, stripe, check or any device on *both* selvedge sides (as frequently patterns are stamped, so that if *one* selvedge only be matched, the opposite one is irregular) ; pin in position. Turn under the weft sides similarly, keeping the corners true to a right angle. Fix

carefully, close to the edge. It sometimes happens, especially in common print, that the pattern is not stamped evenly with the threads; therefore, in fixing the patch, attention must be paid to matching the pattern in preference to keeping the patch by the threads.

6. Hold the patch to the worker, and sew all round on the right side, using cotton the same colour as predominates in the print.

7. Flatten the sewing. Fig. 148 shows the right side appearance.

FIG. 148.—PATCH ON RIGHT SIDE.

8. Turn to the wrong side, and cut away the damaged material and superfluous turnings of the patch, if there be any, to within ⅜ in. of the sewing stitches. (Fig. 149.) A crease is sufficient guide for the cutting, or pins may be used as suggested for flannel patching. This will leave a raw-edged square or oblong, which will need over-casting. The embroidery method or blanket-stitch is usually adopted, which produces a *twist* of cotton at the edge. On *no account* should button-hole stitches be used, which would make a harsh ridge, and appear most unsightly on the right side when the garment is ironed.

Over-casting is worked thus: Hold the patch in position to start at the *top left-hand corner*. Be careful that the stitch does not show through on the right side. Run the cotton down

between the folds, and bring the needle out at the raw edge.
(*A* in Fig. 149.) Hold the cotton under the thumb—put the
needle in at *B, i.e.,* $\frac{1}{8}$ in. from the raw edge, and bring out at

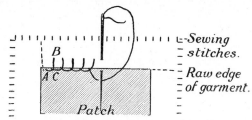

FIG. 149.—WRONG SIDE OF PATCH.

C—8 or 10 *stitches to an inch are ample,* as it is quite unnecessary to spend valuable time upon close stitches providing the
work be neat. Do not pull the cotton too tightly, or the raw
edge will roll under and form a ridge. Put a diagonal stitch

FIG. 150.—JOIN IN OVER-CASTING.

in each corner. A join in over-casting requires care ; to finish
off the old cotton, run the needle up at right angles to the raw
edge in the same direction as the stitch and at the *right*-hand
side of it ; begin with the fresh cotton by running in the reverse

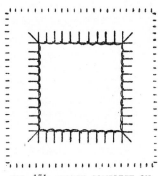

FIG. 151.—PATCH COMPLETE ON
THE WRONG SIDE.

direction at the *left*-hand side and bringing the needle out at
the twist of the last stitch, and in each case slipping the needle
between the folds. (Fig. 150.) Fig. 151 shows the patch
complete on the wrong side.

This method of working the wrong side is the one usually adopted. If preferred, over-casting, such as is used in dressmaking, may be employed in household mending. (Page 107.)

Another method of working the wrong side is as follows : Cut away the damaged material ⅜ in. from the sewing stitches ; mitre the corners of the garment, and cut away the folded corners of the patch, as shown in Fig. 152 ; flatten out and over-cast the garment and the patch separately. This necessitates a double quantity of work, and the corners have no protection other than the over-casting, and are, consequently, insecure, besides the patch being more troublesome to iron. (Fig. 152.)

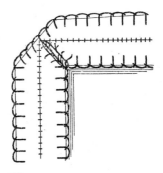

FIG. 152.—ANOTHER METHOD OF TREATING
THE WRONG SIDE.

Second Method of working a patch by which the sewing is on *wrong* side. This requires greater skill in fixing, and if well done, repays for the trouble, as the patch is almost invisible. It is worked thus—

1. Take the piece of print intended for patch, and place it *under* the damaged part, moving it about till the pattern exactly matches. Be sure to leave a good margin of print. Pin the patch and the garment firmly together.

2. Turn the garment to the wrong side, and fold down ⅜ in. of the patch, the right sides on to the wrong (selvedges first). Remove the pins as necessary.

3. Make a diagonal crease through each corner of the garment.

4. Turn to the right side and cut up two of the adjacent creases towards the selvedge side, *just to the corners of the patch*, and not a trifle beyond. The left forefinger on the wrong side will help to limit the point of cutting.

5. Fold under the thin and worn part of garment so that it *exactly* matches the pattern at the edge of the patch.

Hold the folded edges on the wrong side as for sewing.

6. Sew the edges of the garment and the patch together on the wrong side leaving the cotton hanging ; next treat the opposite selvedge by cutting and folding in the same manner, and finally the weft sides.

7. Flatten the sewing.

8. Cut all turnings even on the wrong side rather less than ⅜ in., and over-cast the edges of the garment and the patch by the method shown in Fig. 152.

If a patch be inserted in this way, the over-casting of the garment and the patch must be done separately, and of course, the corners have not the protection they would have if the patch were sewn on the right side ; but this is the plan generally adopted for patches in dresses, and when the work is damped and pressed, the patch should be almost invisible.

IV. Faults liable are—

1. Pattern of print badly matched.

2. Patch puckered.

3. Corners clumsy, insecure and untidy. They should form a right angle.

4. Turning of patch too narrow.

5. Sewing stitches too deep and uneven.

6. Over-casting irregular and too closely worked ; raw edge turned under by pulling cotton too tightly.

The raw edge button-holed—this is a very common mistake.

7. Joins in sewing and over-casting insecure and untidy.

CHAPTER XXXII

HINTS ON THE TEACHING OF PRACTICAL MENDING

THE last three chapters have dealt with calico, flannel, and print patching in the very simple form of a square or oblong arrangement, which merely teaches *correct method*, and is only initiatory to practical mending.

This elementary work is only a step on the ladder, for it must not be thought that, after a few lessons in arranging and working a regular piece of new material called " a patch " over an equally regular piece of material called " a garment," girls have had lessons in what is termed—patching. While such teaching used to fulfil the requirements of the needlework Code when this existed, as far as the *letter* was concerned, it fell very far short of meeting the *spirit* which the framers of the syllabus had in view when suggesting that " practical mending " should be taught. If no further efforts are made to give girls some idea of how to apply the knowledge of the *method* of patching to the work required for practical household use, much of the value of any teaching in patching is almost so much wasted time, beyond the advantage to be derived from the practice of the actual stitches. Two lessons in working square or oblong patches should, as a rule (providing the girls have been well taught), be sufficient for gaining a knowledge of the stitches used, their application to garments, and the method of cutting away the supposed worn material.

In order to teach repairing *successfully and intelligently*, a teacher requires an enthusiasm and interest in needlework somewhat above the average. It is necessary that the teacher should obtain specimens of garments (including as large a variety as possible) which need repairing and for which patching is best suited.

The loan of garments from friends, or from the children's parents (circumstances permitting), can generally be secured if the teacher is willing to take the small amount of trouble which such borrowing involves, viz., the asking, obtaining, taking care of, arranging and supervising the mending, and the return of the work to the rightful owners.

A glance at worn garments is an object lesson in itself as to the parts of a garment which need patching, and it will be easily seen that in hardly any one instance is it advisable to put on a patch which requires *four* sides, as frequently the worn part is near a seam or corner, and more often than not in an awkward place.

In garments which may be very worn, not only is patching necessary, but a portion of the garment, *e.g.*, a corner of a band, or entire band, may need renewing, and then a twofold renovation can be taught.

It is advisable to classify the mending into three groups according as suited to calico, flannel or print methods, and to deal with one kind at a time.

A good selection of worn garments would include several of the following—

Calico Work.

(*a*) A garment, which was thin under the arm near the seam.

(*b*) A similar garment worn into the armhole, or on the shoulder.

(*c*) Knickerbockers worn at the knee in children's garments.

(*d*) A similar pair only fastening at the back with buttons and button-holes, which are broken at the end near the band, or the garment may be thin at the upper part of the leg seam.

(*e*) A boy's shirt worn at the elbow and on the shoulder, the latter the result of the friction of the braces. The cuffs may also need repair, and possibly the bottom of the front opening.

(*f*) A calico or linen sheet worn at the corners where pegged to the clothes line.

(*g*) A linen apron torn at the corner.

Flannel Work.

A vest or shirt worn under the arm.

Print Work or Dress Material.

(*a*) An apron or pinafore torn with a nail or other sharp edge.

(*b*) A blouse torn at the waist at the back and worn under the arm.

NOTE.—The above are only samples of practical work, about which every woman should have a knowledge of the best method of repair.

Damask Patching.

This differs considerably from those patches referred to above, but senior girls who may, from their home surroundings, reasonably be supposed to take a pride in needlework, should be shown the correct method of patching table linen, viz., to fix the patch with a *raw* edge over the worn material on the wrong side and to darn down the edge on to the cloth. The right side, after being cleared evenly of thin or worn material, has the cloth darned similarly on to the patch. If damped and pressed this work should prove most successful. (*See* Chap. XLVI.)

156

Suggested Method for obtaining the Maximum of Class Instruction in Practical Mending in the Minimum of Time.

The circumstances of the children have to enter largely into any scheme of work which may necessitate a small amount of needlework to be completed at home, but many instances could be quoted where very successful exhibits of mending have been the result of short class lessons on the method of working, with practice at home in completing the necessary stitches. Much may be accomplished by the hearty and voluntary co-operation of the elder girls towards attaining skill in practical mending. To achieve the best results it is a necessity that a good tone exist between teacher and pupil, as only under these pleasant conditions can the most useful work of patching be made interesting and attractive.

It must depend upon the size of the class as to the manner in which the demonstration is given. If possible, the girls should be taught in small groups of 8 or 10, or as many as can conveniently stand near to the garment while the teacher explains the process of repair.

Steps in Teaching.

I. Select *good* material (preferably not *new*, and give reasons why to avoid such) for the patching, and as much like the original garment in colour and texture as it is possible to obtain. According to the size of the worn part of the garment, prepare the patch so that it will well cover the surrounding weak material. Show the importance of having the selvedge of the patch continuous with the selvedge of the garment.

II. If a patch is required near a seam, note carefully the kind of seam which has been used in making the garment. Unpick the seam so that it extends a short distance beyond the worn material, always undoing at least an inch more of the stitch which forms the fell, so that neat joins may be made, and to facilitate the fixing.

If a patch is required near a hem or band, the unpicking must reach some little distance beyond the limit to be covered by the patch. The garment should be kept *wrong* side uppermost unless for dress material, when it must be turned to the *right* side.

III. Arrange the patch or patches evenly over the worn material, noting that *the sides of the patch which will adjoin the seam must never be turned down,* and that the patch must extend well over the seam, particularly if the seam is curved, as when shaping it will be necessary to cut away some of the patch to match the original curve. Pin and then tack closely in position, showing the girls how to hold the garment so that the patch is not disarranged, and is kept straight by a thread.

No more can be done at this stage until the working is completed, which must secure the patch to the garment, whether it be felling or herring-boning in the case of calico or flannel, or sewing in the case of dress material only.

IV. The lesson must be resumed at a later date when the girls are ready for the next step. It would be as well to recapitulate what has already been done so far.

The removal of the worn part occupies the most important process in the whole work, as it is at this stage that so many garments are spoiled. The teacher should show the need for sharp scissors, and allow at least two girls to take part in this

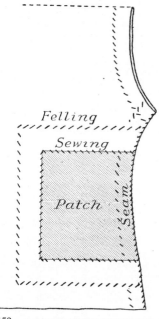

FIG. 153.—A CALICO PATCH UNDER THE ARM.

cutting, after demonstrating how to crease, pin, or define the line where the removal of the worn part should cease. Special stress must be laid on the importance of clearing away the thin material *entirely* at that portion of the work which adjoins the seam or runs into the hem or band. It is in this respect that patching is so often a failure. As a rule, it is necessary to work only *three* sides of a patch, the fourth side being joined into the seam ; sometimes only *two* sides may be required if the patch is near a corner of a garment.

There is occasionally a point of dispute concerning the best place to start the working of the stitches in patching. The most convenient position for the practical work should remove any doubt, viz., *at the edge* and *not* in the middle of a side as is so frequently taught, where the join would be most conspicuous. The rule in all needlework should be to avoid joins

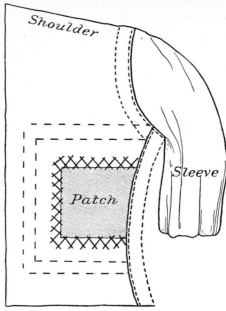

FIG. 154.—A FLANNEL PATCH UNDER THE ARM OF A SHIRT.

in awkward places, and to conceal them as far as is consistent with security.

V. The right side must now be prepared as required for

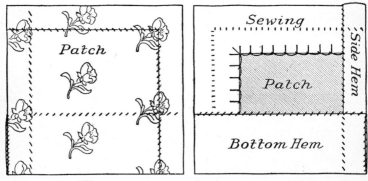

FIG. 155.—A PRINT PATCH AT THE CORNER OF AN APRON.

sewing, or felling may be arranged for very thin material, and it is advisable for muslin or old linen. A run-and-fell seam may be substituted instead of sewing if preferred. There is a tendency to make the seam in calico patching too wide. A good ¼ in., or slightly more in the case of thick material, is sufficient. It is important that the fell of the *seam of the garment and the fell of the patch be as nearly as possible the same width*. In flannel work the raw edges will not require fixing for herring-boning. In print or dress material the wrong side should be made neat by over-casting if it is likely to be exposed, but it is not always possible to get at the wrong side.

Another break must be made in the instruction at this stage while the work suggested in Step V is completed.

VI. The patch has now to be shaped to match the continuity of the *raw edges of the opened* seam or edge, and the mending can be finished by making a seam or hem or band to match exactly the original arrangement on the garment in width and style.

If some such plan can be adopted (even with modifications), *many* garments can be repaired in the course of the year (twenty specimens of mended garments were completed in one instance) with much good to the girls, and much self-satisfaction to the teacher that she has taught " Practical Patching."

A few illustrations are given to show the finished appearance of patched garments. Pieces of material representing " sections of garments " may be substituted for practice purposes.

Fig. 153 shows a calico patch inserted at the under arm of a garment. One side of the patch extends *into* the seam.

Fig. 154 shows a flannel patch under the arm and into the armhole of a flannel shirt. The illustration shows a shirt made by machine in which the side seam and sleeve are stitched. A run-stitched and herring-boned side would be used if the garment were made by hand.

Fig. 155 shows a patch let into the corner of a print pinafore or apron. Both right and wrong sides are shown in order that the *two* sides of the patch may be seen extending into the hems.

NOTE.—Patches in flannelette may be worked either as for wool or cotton, *e.g.*—

(*a*) If the material is very thick and of a firm substance, it may be herring-boned like flannel.

(*b*) If the material is very thin, or of common quality, it should be sewn and felled, or run and felled.

Flannelette should never be *torn* (unless it is exceptionally good), as the threads are strained too much for working purposes.

Stocking-web material which is too worn to admit of darning may be patched as for flannel.

PART III
DARNING

INTRODUCTION.

I. Definition of Darning.—Darning is that art or method (it is *not in itself a stitch*) by which new threads are supplied in place of the thin or worn-out woven ones, being, in fact, the " prevention and cure " of holes ; and to describe it accurately it may be called " hand-weaving," or an imitation of the process adopted in the manufacture of materials.

A definition suited to young pupils might be : Darning is the way by which new threads are put in the place of those which are thin or worn-out. The Kindergarten occupation of " mat weaving " forms an excellent introduction to darning, as it is illustrative of patterns of darning. Some of the specimens might be used by the teacher to illustrate ordinary weaving, showing the perpendicular or warp threads, and the horizontal or weft threads, crossing the warp at right angles, and forming " the pattern " by taking up some of the warp threads, and then missing some.

II. Fundamental Rules for any kind of Darning.

1. If possible, prevent a hole from coming by strengthening a thin place.

2. As a rule, begin at the left-hand side of the part to be darned—

   (*a*) because it is easier to see any pattern that has to be repeated in the darn ; and

   (*b*) the hand does not cover up the darning while it is being worked, neither does it rub over the mending, which might fray it, or tend to make it rough-looking.

3. Do not make a straight edge, such as a square or oblong (*see* Note on p. 167), because all the strain has to be borne by one row of loops, or threads, and another weak place will probably arise in consequence. Any shape which is irregular is good, *e.g.*, a wave edge, a diamond, a rhomboid, or octagonal shape. The latter is to be recommended.

4. Upon washing material leave short loops, to allow for the shrinkage of the mending thread. The loops of the darning should *not* be cut—it is unpractical. No attention

163

need be given to fastening on and off. The ends of the thread should be left hanging and cut even with the loops. The threads of the darning are so woven in with the original material as to make any fastening unnecessary.

5. Use mending thread as much like the original material in colour, texture, size, and stranding as it is possible to obtain.

6. Be careful that whatever the nature of the darn, the mending must not in the slightest degree strain the material, or cause the least pucker. Holding the thumb upon the thread as it is pulled through the material is a great help in keeping the work flat.

CHAPTER XXXII

(a) NEEDLE-THREADING
(b) MANNER OF HOLDING THE WORK
(c) POSITION OF THE NEEDLE

Introduction.—Needles used for darning purposes are longer than ordinary sewing needles. This may be easily accounted for, because several stitches are taken upon the needle in darning. As various kinds of threads are used for mending, *e.g.*, cotton, wool, flax, silk, the darning needle is provided with a long eye, in order that it may easily receive any kind of thread. Wool needles with blunt points are sometimes used for darning on web ; they are shorter than darners, and have a larger eye.

Method of Threading the Darning Needle—

1. Take the thread in the left hand, and hold a short end between the thumb and finger.

2. Hold the needle in the *right* hand, point downwards.

3. Put the shank of the needle to the left of thread, and take the short end of the thread between the thumb and finger as well as the long end (this encloses the needle in a loop).

4. Draw the needle out of the loop, which must be held firmly between the thumb and finger, and so that a little piece of the loop can be seen.

5. Place the eye of the needle on to the loop of thread, and draw the thread through the eye with right-hand thumb and finger.

This method is for Angola or any woollen mending ; other threads can be passed through the needle in the ordinary way.

(b) MANNER OF HOLDING THE WORK.

The material should be held over the first and second fingers, which should be a little distance apart from each other ; the third finger and thumb can then hold the work firmly in place.

(c) POSITION OF THE NEEDLE.

As most of the varieties of darning are formed by rows of thread, worked *from* the chest and *to* the chest, a certain position of the needle is peculiar to each up and down row.

UP ROW, or from the chest.—Place the needle upon first and second fingers of the right hand, and hold in place by the thumb.

DOWN ROW, towards the chest.—Almost as for ordinary stitching, only the thumb and finger cannot be so near the point on account of the length of needle ; the elbow needs keeping up slightly from the side.

CHAPTER XXXIII

FIRST PRINCIPLES OF DARNING

I. Introduction.—The method of darning can be first taught, irrespective of threads, on a coarse, soft flannel. No strain on the eyesight is thereby experienced even by young workers.

II. Directions for Darning.—The diagrams (Fig. 156) illustrate various shapes, and any of these may be selected for beginners. (*See* Note on p. 167.)

About 15 to 20 stitches might be taken in the largest part of the darns, but this depends upon the coarseness of the material.

No. 4 is, perhaps, the most practical; but No. 1 is considered the easiest to teach.

1st Row.—Commence at the bottom left-hand side with the needle pointing *from* the chest, taking up a small piece of material and passing over an equal amount, till as many stitches are on the needle as are needed to form the pattern. Leave an end of cotton about ¼ in., and hold the thumb on the thread while drawing it through.

An explanation should be given to a class as to the reason why no secure commencement or finish is made.

2nd Row.—This will be a little to the right of the last row. The needle will now point towards the chest, and take a stitch just above (or below if the shape of the darn be such) where the cotton came out, and thus will take up the threads which were passed *over* in the preceding row; leave a small loop of cotton, about ⅛ in. (half the length of little finger-nail to a child), and continue the other rows according to the pattern. No fastening off is needed, but the thread is left hanging and cut even with the other loops.

III. Remarks.—Specimens shown to the class will help to impress the mind with the principles mentioned above. It is advisable to use coloured threads for darning. Besides being attractive to a child, it easily shows up any error in darning. Embroidery cotton No. 35 is suitable for practice purposes.

The blackboard should be freely used to illustrate this lesson to a class.

IV. Faults which will occur—
1. Shape badly formed, and irregular rows.
2. Loops not of sufficient length, or too long and uneven.
3. Threads pulled out of position.
4. Darning drawn and puckered in appearance.

V. Note. Many teachers consider the darn sufficiently difficult for young pupils if the same number of stitches are

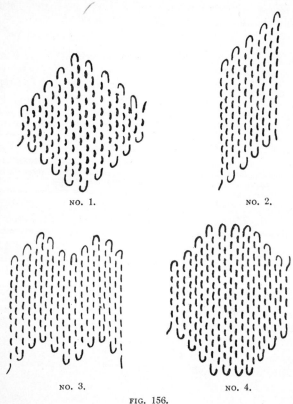

NO. 1. NO. 2.

NO. 3. NO. 4.

FIG. 156.

These diagrams are only intended to illustrate the shapes *of darns and* not the sizes.

kept on the needle throughout the darn, forming either a square or oblong.

Although this method is sanctioned it is not so practical as the shapes shown in Fig. 156.

CHAPTER XXXIV

DARNING A THIN PLACE ON WOOLLEN MATERIAL
e.g., FLANNEL, TWEED, SERGE, etc.

I. Remarks.—A thin place occurs when the " nap " wears off the fabric, leaving the threads bare. A garment may be made to last much longer and look neater, if darned as soon as the weakness is seen, as the object of the darn is to prevent a breaking of threads in the material. For the names of garments, with the parts that need darning in this way, *see* Chapter on " Flannel Patch," Heading II. Instead of " patching," read " darning."

II. Material Used for Mending.—" Wool upon wool " is the principle, therefore Angola, Shetland, or Andalusian wools are all suitable—of course, used singly—and, if too thick, the strand may be untwisted. Flannel is sometimes darned with silk, or flax thread. If dress material has to be repaired, the selvedge ravellings of the stuff form an excellent mending thread, and the darn will then be almost invisible.

III. Directions for Working.—The method employed is similar to the darning described in Chapter XXXIII. It is advisable to read these instructions before commencing to darn. Any of the shapes shown in Fig. 156 are suitable. *As a rule*, it is better to darn *parallel with the selvedge,* and so strengthen the threads which bear most of the strain. The darning is worked upon the wrong side. About ⅛ in. may be taken on the needle and the same amount passed over. Generally the space *between* each row is equal to the size of the stitch, or the rows may be closer if preferred. Loops should be left about $\frac{1}{10}$ in. In the second row, the material *passed over* in the *preceding row* must be taken up. Even distances can be gauged by the eye when the first few rows are started. In some dress materials the style of darning must be regulated by the weave of the material, *e.g.*, upon serge or twilled flannel, a twill darn would look well. Fancy patterns in thin place darning are formed merely by taking up and passing over a certain number of threads.

It is sometimes difficult to darn dress material on the *wrong* side owing to the inconvenience which would be caused in removing the lining. In this case, the work must be done on the *right* side, and no loops should be left, but the thread must be kept rather loose to avoid any puckering.

IV. Points requiring Attention are—

1. That the darning extends sufficiently over the thin place, and that it is upon the *wrong* side of the material, and also the selvedge way.

2. That straight edges are avoided.

3. That the threads taken up and passed over are kept at regular distances in each successive row.

4. That loops are left about ⅛ in. in length.

5. That the darn is not puckered, and that it presents a neat appearance when done.

CHAPTER XXXV

PLAIN DARNING ON STOCKING-WEB AS FOR A THIN PLACE

I. Introduction.—When attempting any kind of darn on webbing, it is essential that an explanation should be given of the formation of the stocking-web, as until its make has been clearly understood, a pupil will not succeed in forming a pattern. The success of any darn on webbing depends upon the right use being made of the loops.

The wearing of underclothing which is made of stocking-web material is gradually becoming more general, so that it is most essential that special attention be given to methods of repair.

II. Description of Web.—The chief feature of the webbing is its *elasticity*, and the aim in darning is to retain this as much as possible.

Cotton stocking-web is woven in three sizes—coarse, medium, fine. The medium web is recommended for practice purposes, and embroidery cotton No. 18 is a suitable thread for darning.

School drapers now stock a woollen fabric in black, tan, and natural colours. It is similar to the web used in the manufacture of merino socks and stockings.

Stocking-web is a *facsimile* of knitting, or to express it literally, " knitting is hand-weaving."

The " hand weaving " of knitting should be compared with the " loom weaving " of the web.

The *right* side of the web represents " plain " knitting and the *wrong* side " purl."

Right Side.—The loops appear in columns, also in rows running from right to left, all of which are linked together ; as this kind of darn is not worked upon the right side, that description is enough for present needs, and it can be treated with more fully in Swiss darning.

Wrong Side.—(Fig. 157.) This also consists of—

1. Columns of Loops.—These are very closely connected with each other ; one column of these loops has an *upward* curve, the loops being turned *away* from the worker ; the next column, either on the right or left, has a *downward* curve, the loops being *towards* the worker. Each of the " up " loops has two " down " ones, which begin from it on either side, and every down loop has two " up " ones coming from it in the same way.

The distinction between these two kinds of loops must

be most strictly observed, and it is of no use to proceed further in teaching until the weaving be understood.

2. Rows of loops going across the web, which seem to form pairs of rows (Fig. 157), curving upwards and downwards alternately; these are also closely joined together.

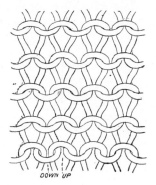

FIG. 157.—WRONG SIDE OF WEB.

III. Material Used.—In learning the method of darning it is usual to work on a piece of flat web, which should be dispensed with as soon as possible, and the actual " round," as for a stocking, introduced. This increases the difficulty in handling and makes the work more practical, as specimens are only illustrative of real garments. A teacher should aim at accomplishing this result successfully, but practice is necessary on flat web. (The point of economy need not be questioned, as several darns can be worked on the circular piece.) Coloured embroidery cotton is best on cotton web for school use, angola mending or any yarn for merino web, worsted for woollen web, knitting silk upon silk web.

IV. Method of Holding a Stocking for Darning.—The position of flat material was described in Chapter XXXII ; for circular web, place the left hand in the round, and arch the fingers so that the supposed garments can be held between the second and third fingers, and the part to be darned stretched across the space between the first and second fingers. The material will be firmer if the lower part of the thin place be grasped with the thumb and first finger.

Some people advise putting a piece of card or stiff paper under the material to be mended, and holding the work as for a flat surface ; as this is unpractical, it is not recommended, as the handling of the soft webbing has eventually to be mastered, but wooden substitutes for the hand are becoming very general. (*See* p. 178, the end of Heading **V**.)

V. Directions for Working.—Darns for thin places are usually worked on the wrong side. An octagonal is the most practical of the irregular shapes, and has the advantage of preparing for the method of darning a thin place which usually surrounds a hole.

1st Row.—" Up " column of loops.

Begin at the left-hand corner of the thin place, take one, miss one, etc., till a sufficient number of loops are on the needle to form the side—leave a short end ($\frac{1}{8}$ in.) which needs no fastening, as the darning forms such a strengthening, that with a first washing the mending thread felts into the webbing and makes the work most secure.

2nd Row.—" Down " column of loops.

These will be in the *next* column, adjoining the first row, so that a column is *not* left between. The first loop taken up in the second row should be the one *just above* where the thread leaves the first row. Take one, miss one, etc., till one more loop is on the needle than in preceding row, which will bring the thread out one loop below that in the first row, but with only *one* more loop in the column. Leave loops about $\frac{1}{8}$ in. (to allow for shrinkage in washing), and hold the thumb on the thread as it passes through the web, which will regulate the length of the loop and keep the work flat.

3rd Row.—As the first, taking up the loop just *below* where the thread leaves the second row, and making the row one loop longer as before.

4th Row.—As the second, still increasing. (Fig. 158.) Continue working thus across the thin place ; if preferred, the same number of loops may be kept on the needle across the centre, then decrease to match the left-hand side.

As soon as a few rows are worked, " the pattern " (if such it can be called) shows in alternate rows of web, which seem to form " pairs," and it becomes easy to detect at a glance if any irregularity breaks the " double row " appearance of the web. If the wrong loops are taken up, the pattern will form a line of three *slanting* loops, and is best unpicked by cutting the last loop of the thread.

On fine webbing such as is often used for socks and stockings, the loops are too small to be dealt with individually, and the needle is passed *through* 2 or 3 loops. The main principles of darning are the same.

VI. Faults met with will be similar to those upon pages 167, 169, and in addition, neglecting to keep the pattern of a plain darn, by combining it with a twill or wave.

VII. Remarks.—To demonstrate darning, a piece of knitting made of thick cotton cord, rug wool or fleecy wool, stretched upon a wooden frame, or even pinned to the blackboard, will be of great assistance in illustrating the formation of the web and the manner of darning.

No teacher should attempt a lesson in darning without some means of demonstrating her subject. Any trouble spent in this respect will be amply repaid by the increased interest of the class, and the successful results obtained.

When a darning lesson is to be given, a diagram of a very coarse piece of webbing should be drawn *before* the lesson and

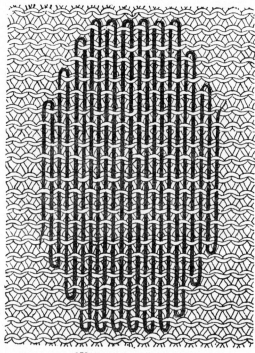

FIG. 158.—PLAIN DARN ON WEB.

The loops should be ⅛ inch in length. The exaggerated appearance of the web seems to make the loops appear somewhat shorter.

used for illustrating. Webbing is not as difficult to draw as it appears at first sight. If a loop be analysed it will be seen that the curves are simple pieces of freehand, and a lined blackboard will prove most helpful in regulating the size of the loops.

CHAPTER XXXVI

MENDING A HOLE IN STOCKING-WEB

COMMON METHOD.

I. Introduction.—This plan merely forms a lattice work over the hole, thereby filling the gap, and making no attempt to imitate the pattern of the web. Practice should have been given upon webbing as for a thin place, before working this method ; in fact, it is useless to attempt to mend a hole unless a thin place can be darned with the utmost regularity.

For teaching purposes, new material has often to be used, and *medium* web is preferable with darning cotton as recommended in Chapter XXXV.

For darning on fine web, such as ordinary merino or cashmere stockings, so much attention cannot be paid to individual loops as would be expected in coarser web, but the principle is the same. (*See* pp. 180 and 181.)

DARNING ON COARSE OR MEDIUM WEB.

In order to give an idea of the method of forming the strands over a hole, it is necessary to actually *cut away* a portion of the web, and not merely to snip one loop and stretch the hole about over the thumb, which is not sufficiently realistic of the holes that usually occur in stockings. The loops may become disconnected, and the hole appear larger than it really is, but it frequently happens that some portion of the tissue is completely worn away, and needs supplying. Unless material is actually cut out in new webbing, it does not teach the mending of a fair-sized hole, such as usually happens in children's hose.

II. Preparation of Material for Darning.—On the right side of the new web, make a perpendicular slit barely $\frac{1}{2}$ in. (not more) in length, and another at *right angles to this, across about four loops*—cut another perpendicular slit at the other end of the horizontal cutting to match the first one in length, and then cut off the loose piece of web. This is *quite* large enough for a darn for any practice purpose, as the hole increases in size very rapidly when it is prepared for working, and a large hole is quite useless for teaching good methods. Still keeping the web upon the right side, clear away with the needle any little fluffy ends that may be in the loops, so that each loop is *clear and distinct*. The loops of the cotton webbing show no tendency to run down and form ladders, as woollen web might do, therefore it is hardly necessary to draw the loops together, but if it is preferred to do so, use an ordinary sewing needle and cotton, and lightly connect the loops, being very careful

174

that the hole is not drawn in the least degree, or the sides will pucker. This stranding is hardly necessary if the hole be handled gently and not " worried " into fraying.

If preferred, the hole may be cut circular in shape, and only the top and bottom of the hole cleared of ends. The method of mending is the same.

III. Method of Darning.—All round the hole a thin place is to be imagined, which it is necessary to strengthen. Hold the material wrong side uppermost in the position described as for

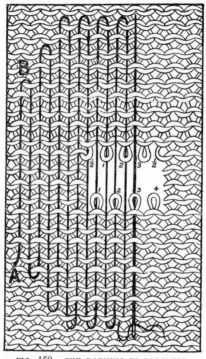

FIG. 159.—THE DARNING IN PROGRESS.

a thin place. About ½ an in. to the *left of hole*, and ½ in. *below* (certainly not more) is ample for strengthening purposes. Commence at A in diagram (Fig. 159), with the up loops; take one, and miss one for ½ in. above the hole (B in diagram). Continue working as for a thin place until the hole is reached; leave loops ⅙ in.

It must be noticed that the loops at the bottom of the hole are *not opposite* the loops in the upper row, but loop *faces space* and *vice versâ*, so that if there are four clear loops at the bottom, there will be three whole loops at the top, and two *half loops*, the *sides* of which will be joined on to the mass of the web.

In crossing the hole, if the needle passes *through a loop in the upper row*, it must follow to the corresponding *space in the lower row*. The teacher's coarse knitting will show very plainly which loops to take up in the mass of the web, and also which *free or loose* loops should be taken on the needle.

The eye can easily tell which of the loops of the thin place, above and below the hole, it is necessary to take up, in order to keep the pattern alternating in the " pairs of rows " as for

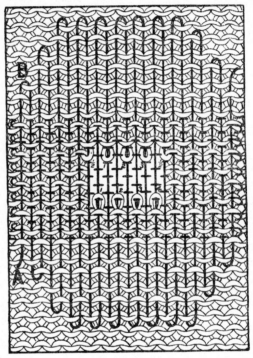

FIG. 160.—HOLE COMPLETE ON THE WRONG SIDE.
(The threads will be quite close together when crossing the hole ; they are spread out in the illustration to show their position.)

the thin place darning. The sides of the hole must not be frayed in the working, but should they do so, the ends may be cut even with the sides of the hole, but no further, as the crossing will secure these frayings to a large extent. Be very careful that the needle passes *through* each free loop, so that it is really connected again by a strand with the loop to which it belongs on the opposite side of the hole. It is wise at every row to look at the right side, and see that the needle has passed clearly *through each loop*, as the loops are inclined to fall outwards on the *right* side, and so the needle is likely to split them. Be careful not *to contract* the hole in stranding across it, but leave the thread sufficiently loose to keep the work flat. It is well to increase each row in length till about ⅓ of the width of the hole is stranded, then work over the centre without increasing, and decrease on the right-hand side to correspond with the left. This completes the warp darning, and forms a stranding upon which to work the lattice.

IV. Crossing the Hole.—Bend the work round so that what previously formed the top and bottom, is at the right and left hand respectively. The hole will need strengthening for a *good* ¼ *in. above and below it.* The mending thread alone should be taken up. It will be seen that the plain darn at the sides of the hole has a double row of loops of the web showing. If Fig. 158 be held sideways at a distance from the worker, this double row of loops can be easily seen. The strand which should be taken up now is the one *between* these two rows, and the rows must be *pushed* apart with the darning needle. Begin at the required distance from the hole, and take up one strand and miss one all across the darn ; in the second row, take up the thread missed in the preceding row, which is a long thread and quite easy to get at, and so on, catching in any jagged edges, and taking care that in crossing the hole, the lattice is perfectly formed by taking

FIG. 161.—HOLE COMPLETE ON RIGHT SIDE.

up each alternate thread. There is a tendency to split the strands in crossing, and consequently spoil the appearance of the darn on the right side ; this must be guarded against, and the eye of the needle used if the darn cannot be crossed properly without. (Fig. 161.) Some teachers advise starting the crossing from the middle of the hole.

If sewing cotton has been used to connect the loops, it should now be cut and withdrawn.

FINE WEB DARNING.

V. Method of Mending.—When looking over socks and stockings returned from the laundress, it is not unusual to find, besides several thin places caused by friction with the boot, a few holes, which may have been the result of one loop having given way, run down, and so formed a ladder.

A hole of this description had better be treated as follows—

On the right side. take up the ladder according to one of the methods described in Chapter XLII, and draw the hole together with sewing cotton, " lacing " it, as it were, so that the loops are as much as possible in their original position—be very careful that no puckering is caused—turn to wrong side, and darn as for a thin place.

A hole of this kind rarely requires crossing, or only slightly.

Upon very fine web, two loops may be taken on needle and two missed, or even more. It is most essential that all thin places be darned. Holes are filled similarly to coarser web.

Frequently holes are repaired by ignoring the loops—the " take up " and " pass over " of the material being dealt with as though the loops did not exist. Busy housewives invariably mend in this fashion, and a good darn can be worked providing the needle and thread are not too thick.

Occasionally in children's stockings one meets with a " huge gaping space " with " bits " of the broken tissue hanging loose. It is a help towards getting the stocking shapable, if a piece of stiff paper, or card, be placed in the stocking, as puckering will be less likely while lacing the hole—do not cut the loose ends, but draw them straight in place while connecting the sides of the hole. Fabric worn away in this manner should be supplied as in the directions for darning coarser web.

Some people use a shaped ball, made of wood or bone, and employ it as a substitute for the hand inside the sock or stocking, for the purpose of having a firm substance to darn upon.

Pieces of wood in the shape of a mushroom can be bought for a few pence.

VI. Points for Criticism—

1. Mending thread either too coarse or too fine for the web, so that it makes a botch, or is too weak to answer its purpose.

2. Hole itself badly prepared ; conspicuous by its size—being too large, or not of sufficient size to show a fair amount of darning.

3. Thin web surrounding the hole not sufficiently strengthened, or too much darning in comparison with the size of the hole (a common fault).

4. Irregular pattern in plain darning.

5. Neglecting to pass the mending thread *through* the loops, when stranding across the hole.

6. Stranding too loose or puckered.

7. Loops at edge of darn too long, or omitted entirely.

8. Shape of darn unsuitable to the size of the hole.

9. Crossing uneven, and the lattice-work not kept correctly to the proper threads.

10. General appearance puckered or bulky.

CHAPTER XXXVII

A THREE-CORNERED TEAR, HEDGE TEAR, OR CATCH TEAR

I. Description.—The above are all names for the same kind of rent. This tear usually happens in dress material, though sometimes in linen or calico. It is caused by catching the garment on some sharp surface, such as a nail or edge of a desk (hence its importance to teachers).

As a rule, the material tears *with the threads*, the corner at *A* being often jagged and ravelled, as this is the place where, in tearing, the strain was the greatest, and it not unfrequently happens that the stuff is so much damaged that a piece of material is quite torn away. For the sake of appearance and for teaching the method of working the darn, it is best to make the sides of the tear the same length (say, ¾ in. or 1 in.) (Fig. 162) ; but in a " real " tear, more

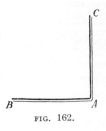

FIG. 162.

often than not, the *selvedge threads* give only a little (being the stronger), and the *weft threads* tear some distance, and are more frayed and irregular.

II. Material Used.—For the sake of giving an exact idea as to method of mending, it is well to practise a few rows of darning as for a thin place (p. 171) on an even-threaded flannel (Yorkshire is the best), and ultimately upon dress material.

The mending thread will depend upon the kind of stuff which needs darning. Darns upon any linen fabric should be worked with flax or flourishing thread, about the same size strand as the material is made of. Fine embroidery cotton is also suitable. On woollen material, fine angola or silk exactly matching in colour may be used, but if any difficulty arises in matching the shades, as might happen in fancy fabrics, the *selvedge* ravellings of the stuff are excellent for the purpose, if a sufficient length can be obtained. A darn can be exquisitely managed by this latter means and rendered almost invisible, and it is to be preferred to any kind of mending material.

III. Preparation for Mending.—For practice purposes, where the tear has to be made, it is best done by putting the point of the scissors into the material, making a slit about ¾ in. in

179

length, and another at right angles to the end of the first one. If the stuff is inclined to fray it is advisable to fasten the material to be darned, wrong side uppermost, either upon a piece of paper or card, as this makes a firm substance to darn upon ; besides, puckering is less likely to occur. It is sometimes well to draw the edges of the tear together gently, so that the threads may become as continuous as possible. This is occasionally an advantage, but is not advised for children's practice, and if chosen, very fine sewing cotton must be used —a hair from the head is an excellent substitute on dark dress material, being strong and yet fine.

There are two ways of drawing edges together, according as the material is thin and loose, or of a firm texture.

For Thick Material. This method is similar to Fig. 167, only the stitches should not be so close together. The needle is brought out at about ⅛ in. from the edge, and then inserted *into the slit* and brought out ⅛ in. from the edge on the opposite side of the tear—pass the needle again into slit and so on.

For Thin Material. Begin at the left-hand side, about ⅛ in. from the edge, pass the needle to the back of the work, and bring it out ⅛ in. on the opposite edge—hold the left thumb upon the raw edges while drawing the cotton through—insert the needle a short distance to the right from where the cotton came out, and bring it out on the opposite edge on a line with the commencement, and so on. This method of drawing together has the advantage of keeping the frayed edges up on the wrong side, that is, on the darned side. The stitches need to be removed very carefully when the darn is finished.

IV. Method of Mending.—The darn is worked, *as a rule*, on the wrong side (*see* p. 183. V). Begin the darning weft way of the material, and hold the tear so that the warp threads lie along the finger. The shape of the darn is shown in Fig. 163, and is suitable for materials of medium thickness.

1. Commence at the left-hand side about ⅜ in. to the left of B (this distance is usually sufficient protection), and about ⅜ in. above the tear. Take *two* threads and miss *two*

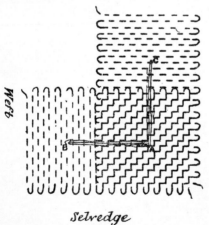

Selvedge

FIG. 163.—FOR MATERIALS OF MEDIUM THICKNESS.

in a line with the threads of the stuff for about ⅜ in. below the tear. Be very careful to keep the thumb upon the raw edges while the thread is drawn through, as this will help to prevent ravelling as well as keeping the darn flat.

2. Leave two clear threads between each row, and take up in the second row the threads missed in the preceding one, keeping the same number of stitches on the needle in each row. On materials where threads cannot be easily seen, take up a small piece of material, say $\frac{1}{8}$ or $\frac{1}{10}$ in., and pass over a proportionate amount, leaving the same between each row. This plan is almost compulsory on dress fabrics and the most practical.

3. On washing material leave loops about $\frac{1}{8}$ in. in length to allow for shrinking. This amount is hardly necessary on a non-washing dress material, but just sufficient length so that the darn is kept flat, and without the least sign of dragging.

In crossing the edges of the tear the needle may chance to come out *exactly* in the slit, and so take up the edges by passing *under* them in one row, and *over* them in the next, or it is possible that the needle may end just on one side of the tear, so that the strand will *cross over both edges* in one row, and *under both edges* in the next.

4. Continue darning in this manner for about *three-quarters of the way across the tear*. Unthread the needle.

5. Turn the work round and darn the selvedge way of stuff. Begin at the same distance from the end of the tear as in the previous darning, keeping the same proportion on the needle as before. Work *three-quarters of the way* over the tear.

It sometimes happens that the selvedge and weft threads of the material are not of the *same* thickness, and consequently *the depth* of the weft darning will appear somewhat narrower than the selvedge. It is advisable to keep the depth of the darning to match the weft side, so that another stitch may be necessary on the selvedge side; but this being only for appearance, would not be required on an *even-threaded* material, such as should be used for teaching, so that this suggestion is quite by the way.

6. Now go back to the weft side and resume the darning, carrying it beyond the tear till it is even with the outermost edge of the darning on the opposite way of the stuff. The needle must actually take up *the material* in crossing, so that the stitches show through clearly on the *right* side. Darning a portion of *each side* alternately keeps the mending flatter and the corresponding edges of the tear in place, and so makes a more successful darn.

The pattern may form in crossing one of the ways indicated in Fig. 164. The first method makes a series of steps : in this case the needle goes *into the same place* with each way of the darning, whereas in the other plans, it either *passes over or under the threads, or by the side.*

FIG. 164.—DIFFERENT METHODS OF CROSSING A DARN.

7. Complete the unfinished side, and continue as far as the edges of the other darning threads. When working over the slit, the strand of cotton must be taken up on the needle in one row, and passed over in the next, as in filling up a hole, and any loose threads of material darned into place so that they again form part of the original weaving.

A slightly different plan for an L-shaped darn, and which is specially recommended for *thin* material, is worked as follows—

Carry out the directions on page 181 to the end of paragraph 5.

6. Resume the darning of the selvedge side and carry the thread beyond the limit of the tear, till it is even with the outermost edge of the darning on the opposite way of the stuff.

7. Darn the weft side similarly, following the same plan.

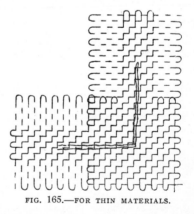

FIG. 165.—FOR THIN MATERIALS.

The diagram (Fig. 165) shows exactly how the working appears. When finished, the double darning will extend over the length of the *sides* of the tear as well as at the corners.

When the work is complete, the double darning will come just where it is needed most, viz., at the jagged corner, which is the weakest place.

V. Finishing Off.—Remove the work from the paper, if it has been used, and cut off any loose threads that there may be, and if noticeable, take out the stitches that held the fractured edges together. The appearance of a darn on dress material is greatly improved if a damp cloth be laid upon the wrong side of the darn and a warm iron pressed upon it. This should not be done on linen fabric, but smacking the darn smartly on the palm of the hand, and then placing it between the leaves of a book, is generally effectual in flattening it.

If a tear happens in a dress where it is impossible to get at the wrong side, the darn may be worked on the *right* side, but no loops should then be left, and the darn needs the greatest care.

ANOTHER METHOD of darning a hedge tear is to form two squares or oblongs of darning over the edges of the tear. This process

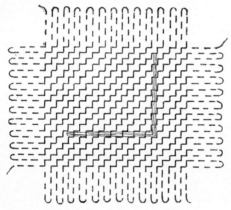

FIG. 166.—FOR ANY KIND OF MATERIAL.

involves a deal more darning than there is any necessity for, consequently takes longer to darn, is no more effectual, and renders a tear on dress material clumsy, as it makes much of what is really very little, and which should be as invisible as possible.

Fig. 166 gives an illustration of the shape.

ANOTHER METHOD of mending a tear in *thick* woollen material or cloth when there happens to be a clean cut, is shown by Fig. 167.

It is a stitch which laces the edges together and is a very strong way of joining two selvedges or edges which are not likely to fray much. The threads cross *between* the edges, and so the join produced is perfectly flat, and if strong, fine thread is used, the mend is nearly invisible after damping and ironing. The stitch is sometimes called "fishbone" pattern.

The needle is run along for about ½ an inch parallel with the cut (which should be held between the finger and thumb of the left hand) and brought out at the left-hand end of the slit ⅛ in. from the edges. The needle is then inserted into the slit and brought out ⅛ in. on the opposite edge, and so on, alternating the position of the needle. As a rule, ⅛ in. is sufficiently close for the stitches, but this depends upon the material—the closer the stitches, the more upright they appear. Several stitches are needed in the corner.

FIG. 167.—A METHOD OF MENDING
A CUT IN CLOTH, SUITABLE
FOR THICK MATERIAL.

A worn place in the elbow or the under arm of a dress can be neatly mended by having a piece of the same material laid under it to strengthen it, and then any jagged ends firmly darned down. It is best to unpick the seam of the sleeve and place the new piece between the lining and the fabric, darning the two materials neatly and flatly together, and then stitching up the seam again.

The knees and seats of boys' trousers may be treated in the same way.

VI. Points requiring Attention are—

1. That suitable mending thread be used.

2. That the darning extends sufficiently over the weakest part of the tear, and that the shape is in proportion.

3. That all loose ends are drawn in place.

4. That *very* short loops are left at the edges.

5. That the weft crossing takes up the *original* material, not merely the mending thread.

6. That the darn is not puckered nor clumsy, but the tear effectually mended, and that the work presents a neat, flat appearance when complete.

CHAPTER XXXVIII

CROSS, DIAGONAL, OR BREAKFAST CUT

I. Introduction.—The above are the names by which a cut in damask linen is usually known. It is generally the result of the careless use of a knife, which cuts both warp and weft threads, and in consequence, requires careful darning. It may occur on a tablecloth at *any angle*, thus—

It is sometimes the diagonal of a square, hence its name, and for teaching the method of working it should be cut thus, although nine cuts out of ten would probably be at some other angle, but principles should be taught first and supplemented by practical work. The usefulness of this kind of darn is often questioned by teachers. It is said that " it is of no use to girls in after life." That these kinds of cuts happen sometimes every one will allow, and also that it is necessary to repair the slit made, or frequent washing will soon make an unsightly hole. Good housekeepers take great pride in keeping table linen neatly repaired, and even if a busy mother cannot find time to mend the linen herself, she will feel the advantage of " knowledge is power," if she can at least superintend and teach another how it should be done. Another objection often raised against the working of a cross-cut darn is " that it is likely to injure the eyesight." If it be taught by a single thread process on fine linen, where the darning is made the chief feature, and the repair of the cut counts for nothing, no doubt this may be true ; but a darn of this kind is not required, but such a one as is suitable to the actual cut in a cloth.

The darn should be worked on *coarse* linen as a preliminary for the damask, so that pupils may be familiar with the correct method of working a darn for this kind of cut. Children would value it more highly if permitted to try their skill on damask, when successful on coarse linen. The difficulty in obtaining old table linen may be met by buying very coarse, new material, and washing it—the cost would be trifling—and the practical value of the lesson so much enhanced.

The lesson should be preceded by a preliminary practice on darning as for a thin place on material (p. 168), as this

185

somewhat simplifies the working of a cross-cut—a few rows of darning would be sufficient.

II. Material Needed.—The method of working is best taught upon coarse linen or Saxony cloth *with a cut*, and finally upon table linen. Any kind of darning cotton will answer the purpose for teaching, but proper linen thread should be used for the damask. It is glossy, and is called " flax " or " flourishing " thread. It can be bought in various sizes suited to the threads of the linen. Coloured thread is recommended for teaching. A fine darning needle (No. 7 or 8) should always be used.

III. Preparation for Darning.—The cut should be *cleanly* made (not jagged) and with very sharp scissors. If the material is creased diagonally each way, and left folded in the triangular form, the scissors can make *one* snip on the crease ($\frac{1}{4}$ in.), which, when opened, will show a cut $\frac{1}{2}$ in. in length (sufficiently long for practice purposes). Some people advise drawing the lips of the cut together with very fine cotton before working the darn ; this is optional and not advised, but if it be done it should be as follows : Put the needle in about $\frac{1}{8}$ in. from the raw edge, pass it under the cut to $\frac{1}{8}$ in. on the other side of the cut ; insert needle a little distance from the place where thread comes out, and pass needle to the other side of cut ; by this means all the raw edges are kept upon the *wrong* side. If preferred, the edges may be drawn together, as recommended *for thick material* on page 180. These threads can be cut out when the darn is completed, but their removal so frequently spoils the appearance of the work that they are better omitted. As both warp and weft threads are cut, the mending threads supplied must be darned warp and weft way.

There are several methods of planning the shape of the darn—

1. By folding creases, generally considered the best.

2. Marking the shape of the darn with pencil.

3. By the aid of pencilled dots.

The first is the most practical and the simplest ; pencilling is not advisable on material, especially for children's use and should be discouraged.

To arrange the folding—

1. Make a sharp crease, *weft* way of the material, and quite straight by the threads, about $\frac{1}{8}$ in. above the end of the cut. (Fig. 168.) Crease (1) in diagram.

2. Make a second crease at *right angles* to the first fold, $\frac{1}{8}$ in. from the other end of the cut. It will depend upon the

slope of the cut—*right to left*, or *left to right*—as to which way this crease is made, whether at the *right*-hand side or the *left*, but it must always be folded so that the *angle formed by the meeting of the folds* (Letter A in diagrams) *is the apex of a triangle of which the cut is the base.* If this be clearly understood, a cut in any position can be correctly darned. It should be noted that point *A* is *opposite* the cut, and *not on a line with it*, as it would be if the *second* crease were made at the wrong side.

The diagrams will illustrate the folding. (Fig. 168.)

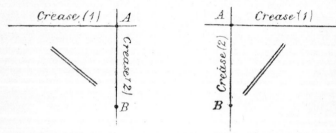

FIG. 168.—SHOWING THE CREASES WITH THE CUT FROM LEFT TO RIGHT.

FIG. 169.—SHOWING THE CREASES WITH THE CUT FROM RIGHT TO LEFT.

IV. Directions for Working.

1. Always darn on the wrong side.

2. Begin at the apex of the triangle *A* (the *meeting place* of the creases gives the *starting place* for the darning).

3. Take 2 threads upon the needle ($\frac{1}{8}$ in. on damask), and miss 2, till letter *B* is reached—which can be found by continuing the *direction of the cut* on to the crease in the mind's eye—count the number of *stitches* on the needle, and take *exactly the same number again below B* (supposing there are 7 stitches from *A* to *B*, 14 stitches will be the number in all for the first row). This line (A B C in Fig. 170) must be carefully done, as it forms the key to the entire darn, and if the distance between B and C is taken too short, the symmetrical appearance of the darn is quite spoiled.

4. The second row will begin 2 threads (or the distance of a stitch) from the first row, and 2 threads higher up, *slanting in the direction of the cut*, or, in other words, the darning is *raised* in each row *towards the cut*, as by this means the material which was *passed over* in the preceding row, will be *taken on* the needle now. There should be the *same* number of stitches on the needle in every row. Leave *short* loops ($\frac{1}{8}$ in.) to keep the work flat, as linen shows very little tendency to shrink.

188

5. Darn across the cut, and continue the strengthening to Crease (3), which must now be made, and is distant from Crease (2) *by the length of the space between A and B* (this can be measured with a piece of paper or inch tape), as the cut when finished will be enclosed *in a square*, the sides of which are all regulated by the space between A and B. Care must be taken to keep the raw edges of the cut on the *wrong* side, and to prevent fraying, which may be avoided if the thumb be kept upon the edges while the thread is drawn

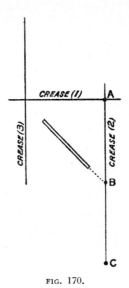

FIG. 170.

through.   The darning when finished will appear in the shape of a rhomboid, *an equal amount of strengthening above and below, and on either side of the cut.* (Fig. 171.) This completes the warp darning.

6. The material should now be turned round, and darned across the weft way.

Fig. 164, on page 182, shows different ways of arranging the weft darning. The paragraph above the diagram gives an explanation of the method. The first plan is shown on the cross-cut (Fig. 173), and is the simplest.

7. Commence at, A, *i.e., exactly the same place* as for the warp darning, taking the same number of threads (or amount of material) on the needle, and leaving the same between each row. Be careful that the needle *takes up the material, not* merely the darning thread, so that the stitches in the crossing show *through clearly on the right side.* When crossing over the

cut, the strand which is taken up in one row must be passed over in the next, so as to form a lattice work, just as if mending a hole in a stocking.

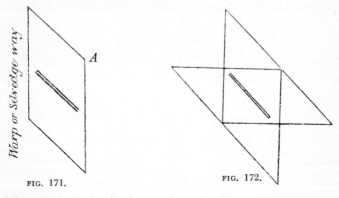

FIG. 171.

FIG. 172.

When the weft darning is complete, the shape of the darn and its general appearance should be as shown in Figs. 172 and 173. It will be noticed that the darning has formed two triangles,

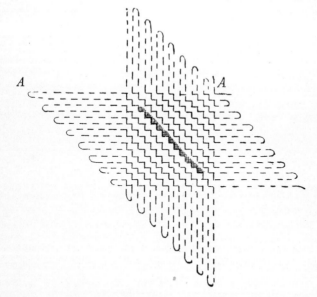

FIG. 173.—DARN COMPLETE ON THE WRONG SIDE.

the apex of one fitting into the base of the other with the cut running in the same direction as the bases, and also *parallel with the loops.*

If the cut is *not* the diagonal of a square, the second crease is folded and the distance A B calculated *just as though the cut had been made in the diagonal crease*, so that the working is the same, only the cut will *not* appear parallel with the loops when finished, although it will be in a square of crossed darning. The darning is sometimes worked in the shape of two triangles instead of as described. The result is the same.

V. Faults met with are—

1. Unsuitable mending material, both in texture and quality.

2. Material folded incorrectly, so that the darning is the wrong shape, according to the direction of the cut.

3. Darning too closely worked—*one* thread only being taken up.

4. Stitches not kept distinctly and evenly to warp and weft threads.

5. Insufficient crossing over the cut, or want of strengthening at the ends.

6. Rough edges of the cut frayed unnecessarily in working, and ends not kept on the wrong side.

7. Weft thread crossing taking up only the new warp thread, instead of the *original* material.

8. Loops not left, or too long, so as to render darn unsightly.

9. Darning thread drawn too tightly, and so producing a puckered appearance.

VI. Remarks.—Another form of darning a cut is shown in Fig. 178. The dotted figure shows the outline of the darning.

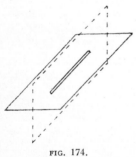

FIG. 174.

This method takes much less time to darn, and the amount of mending is quite sufficient protection to the edges of the cut ($\frac{1}{4}$ in. margin may be allowed). On this account it recommends itself for household purposes, and is infinitely to be preferred to the shape described in detail.

In the illustration the dotted rhomboid is the selvedge darning and the lined rhomboid the weft way. Creases should be made to assist the formation of the shape.

Thin places in damask are darned as described on page 168.

CHAPTER XXXIX

VARIETIES OF DARNS ON WEB, viz., TWILL, WAVE, BIRD'S-EYE

TWILL DARN.

I. Introduction.—This is a simple and very strong way of darning a thin place, not only on webbing, but upon any material which has a twill pattern. Fig. 175 gives an illustration of the method of working. The same number of loops are kept on the needle throughout, by decreasing at the top of the darn and increasing at the bottom, or *vice versâ*.

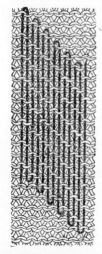

FIG. 175.—TWILL DARN.

Loops appear rather short in the upper part of the diagram ; they should be ¼ inch in length.

II. Directions for Working.—According to Fig. 175—

1st Row.—"Up" column of loops. Take one, miss one, according to the size of the place to be darned.

2nd Row.—"Down" loops. Begin by taking one loop below the preceding row, keeping the same number of loops on the needle as before.

3rd Row.—Take one loop lower, and so on.

It will be seen that the loops in the same horizontal line are taken up only in every fourth row.

It is a pity that this darn is not more often used, as on account of its strength it is to be recommended and it is an easy pattern to follow.

WAVE DARN.

This is similar to the twill, perhaps slightly more difficult.

The illustration shows the pattern commenced with " down " loops. (Fig. 176.)

FIG. 176.—WAVE DARN. (SEE NOTE TO FIG. 179.)

Work a few rows (say five) as for a twill darn ; then reverse the order of the slope of the loops by taking the next loop, either above or below where the thread came out, according to the direction of the first series of rows ; work *one* row less than in first wave (in this case, four) ; change again and darn as for the first slope, and so on.

BIRD'S-EYE.

This darn is rarely used, but the pattern is not difficult to master if worked on coarse webbing, as it so frequently repeats itself, and the eye can detect almost at a glance which loop to take to form the diamond. (Fig. 177.)

Directions for working the darn in the illustration are as follows—

1st Row.—Take one, pass four, etc., take one.

2nd Row.—Take one, pass three, *take two ; pass three ; repeat from*, take one.

3rd Row.—Take one, *pass two, take one, pass one, take one ; repeat from*, pass two, take one.

4th Row.—Take one, pass one, *take one, pass two, take one, pass one ; repeat from*, take one.

5th Row.—Take two, *pass three, take two ; repeat from*.

6th Row.—As the first.

7th Row.—As the 5th, and so on, working backwards.

Remarks.—These darns are all suitable for strengthening the heels and toes of new socks and stockings, commonly called " running."

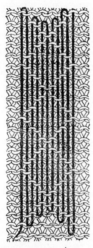

FIG. 177.—BIRD'S-EYE DARN. (SEE NOTE TO FIG. 179.)

If treated in this way they will last twice as long before needing repair.

Heels.—For strengthening a heel, start at the seam loop, and make this the longest line of darning, decreasing gradually on either side. The ball of heel should also be darned.

Toes.—Begin at left-hand side of toe, increase gradually over the centre, and decrease on the right-hand side to match.

It is well to darn both upper and under parts.

Knees.—It is time well spent if the knees of boys' stockings are run before the web gets thin.

CHAPTER XL

SWISS DARNING

I. Definition.—Swiss darning is that method of strengthening a *thin* place (not a hole) in stocking-web material, by exactly covering the loops of the original knitting or weaving with a thread which thickens the loops, while at the same time preserving the elasticity of the web, and rendering the mending almost invisible.

It is preferable to the ordinary darn on account of its neatness and strength, and with a little practice can be as quickly worked, especially on moderately coarse webbing.

The wearing of woven-web (stockinette) underclothing is becoming more general every year, and as the garments are somewhat expensive if of good quality, it is necessary that every care be given to the repair. Friction wears webbing thin very quickly, and Swiss darning forms the best possible means of preserving the web and at the same time retaining the neat appearance of the garments, so that careful workers will not begrudge the time spent in acquiring and applying the stitch, as there are still a few people to be found who realize the importance of taking care of good clothing by preventing holes from making a too premature appearance.

II. Articles upon which a Swiss Darn is Suitable—

1. Any part of a knitted sock or stocking, chiefly knees and legs of boys' stockings, and heels if shoes are worn.

2. Elbows of jersey suits or bodices.

3. Knitted or woven petticoats, vests, combinations, coats cardigans, jumpers and dresses.

4. Gentlemen's pants and sweaters.

5. The sides of a knitted or woven patch may be strengthened by this means.

6. The fingers of knitted gloves.

III. Material Used.—In order to make the darn almost imperceptible, it is necessary to have the mending thread as much like the thread of the article to be mended, both in colour and texture, as it is possible to obtain it. It is an advantage, perhaps, if it be a *trifle* finer, as the darn will be less bulky.

Cotton mending should be used upon cotton web, and wool upon woollen web. Contrasting colours are preferable for learners. A wool needle is recommended, being less likely to split the threads of the loops, but darning needles can be used.

IV. Description of the Webbing.—Before commencing a darn of this kind, it is necessary that the formation of the web be understood, otherwise there may be a difficulty in working a Swiss darn properly.

The *wrong* side of the web was dealt with under the heading of Plain Darning (p. 170).

On the *right* side, the loops appear in *columns* or ribs, also in *rows* running from right to left. If any loop in the mass of web be examined by itself, it seems to consist of two sides (often compared with little leaves) meeting in the loop above and below it. It takes two of these leaves to form one loop, which slopes *upwards*, but if another half loop be added, so as to make three horizontal leaves, a *downward* loop is formed as well (Fig. 178), so that each loop in completing itself forms part of another.

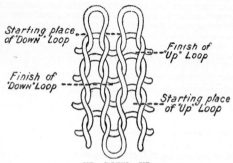

UP   DOWN   UP
FIG. 178.—RIGHT SIDE OF WEB.

Before going further, a student should be able to readily distinguish the " up " loops from the " down," and also be able to bring out the needle quickly at the " starting place " and " finish " of these loops, as all the mistakes that arise are due to a misunderstanding as to the exact position of one loop with regard to its neighbour.

V. Method of Working.—Swiss darning is worked upon the right side, and always horizontally from right to left.

Figs. 181 and 182 show the darning commenced at the *bottom right-hand corner* of the supposed thin place.

To Commence.—Leave a finger length of thread on the wrong side, which must be darned down neatly when the work is finished. Do not pull the thread tightly.

The loops mentioned above are represented in the diagram by slightly curved lines, which, for simplicity, are numbered, and started with " up " loops. (Fig. 179.)

1. Bring the needle out in No. 1 at the right-hand lower corner of the thin place, being the *bottom* or starting place of the *upward* loop, and one of the points where the leaves seem to meet.

2. Follow the *upward right-hand slanting thread*, 1, 2—insert the needle at 2, and take a horizontal stitch under the threads or rib to 4. (Fig. 179.) This will cover *half a loop*.

FIG. 179.—DIAGRAM OF A ROW OF WEBBING.

Care must be taken that the needle does actually follow the woven thread *from the start to the finish*, or where it seems to lose itself in the loop above it, as there is a tendency not to take the stitch sufficiently high, and so only partly cover up the loop.

3. Put the needle back in the same place from which the thread started, and take another horizontal stitch from 1 to 3. This covers the second half of the " up " loop.

4. In at 4 out at 6 ; in at 3 out at 5 ; and in this manner across the thin place. Be careful to finish the row with a *complete* loop, not merely a half one. It will be seen that the needle goes into each loop *twice*, so that *each* loop has *two* parts, and this must be remembered in counting the number worked. The thread on the wrong side will appear somewhat like two lines of running, and it must be noticed that the stitches are all worked in the *same horizontal* line of loops.

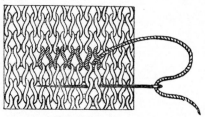

FIG. 180.—TURNING A CORNER.

To Turn a Corner so that the Sides of the Darn are Kept Straight.—Completely finish one row—turn the work round so that what previously formed the bottom of the darn now becomes the top, with the supposed thin place *below* the worked line—bring the needle out *exactly in the middle* of the *last* stitch (which apparently is the *first* now) and it will be at the *starting place* of a " down " loop—the cotton is then in readiness to go on with the second row, which begins with a " down " loop and is worked exactly like the first row, only that the needle is put *into the middle* of the last worked stitch in the previous row each time. (Fig. 180.)

It is advisable to keep the needle almost upright as the column of web is taken up, so as to cover the fabric *entirely*, and not to permit the original web to show through, which it has a tendency to do, and particularly if too fine a mending thread be used.

Completely finish the second row—turn the work round with the finished rows downward—bring out the needle *in the middle* of the last stitch at the *starting place* of an " up " row, which will be like the first and locked into the second. A regular darn (square or oblong) must always be worked first, till the stitches can be freely made, and the corners accurately turned, and so that familiarity is gained with the web.

To Join and Finish.—Pass the needle to the wrong side, and darn down all ends as for plain darning.

The darn may be begun *at the top* and worked downwards. In this case, the *down* part of the loop will be taken first instead of the upward thread, as shown in Fig. 181.

FIG 181.—A SWISS DARN WITH REGULAR SIDES.

Irregular Figures should be practised, *e.g.*, diamond, rhomboid, hexagon, octagon, lozenge or coin-shape, etc., as any darn, to be successful, should never have a straight edge, which would cause an undue strain on one set of already weak loops. The eye will soon detect the place where it is necessary to bring out the needle in order to produce the required irregular shape, and directions are given below, according to the illustration in Fig. 186, which shows a darn complete.

To Turn the Irregular Corners—

Second Row. Completely finish the first row, turn the work round (and the diagram), bring the needle out *one* row down (at the *starting place* of an " up " loop), and exactly underneath the outside point of the last worked stitch, follow the direction of the thread, and work the line, when there should be one more *complete* loop (formed by the two half loops on either side) than in the first row.

Third Row. Turn the work round, bring the needle out mid-way in the length of the last stitch, and outside it, which will be at the *starting place* of an " up " loop, and when the stitch is worked will be *half-a-loop* to the *right* of the previous line; the row, when finished, should contain one more complete loop than the last.

All even rows are worked like the second.

All odd rows are like the third.

If preferred, the darn may have straight sides near the centre, and then be decreased to match the commencement.

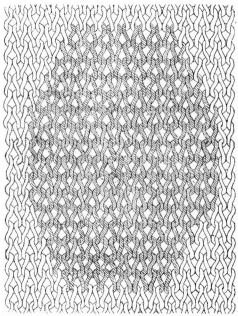

FIG. 182.—AN IRREGULAR SWISS DARN COMPLETE.

VI. Points needing care—

1. That the darning thread is suitable, and that it exactly *covers the original web.*

2. That the thread is kept moderately loose, so as to preserve the elastic character of the web, and to prevent any puckering.

3. That each loop is locked in the last row of loops.

4. That the loops in the same horizontal line are kept even throughout the row.

5. That all ends are darned in neatly on the wrong side.

CHAPTER XLI

GRAFTING

I. Definition.—Grafting is that method by which two pieces of webbing are connected together in such a manner as to produce an invisible join, if the thread used be of the same size, colour, and texture as the original material.

To graft, means to insert a foreign substance in order to strengthen or support, and it is this sense in which it is used in needlework.

II. Uses to which it may be Applied.—It can only be worked upon webbing, either knitted or woven.

1. Joining a new foot, or a portion of one, to an old leg.

2. Finishing off the toe of a knitted sock or stocking. This is an exceedingly neat method, as a ridge is avoided, and the toe rendered so much more comfortable for wear. The toe would be grafted by pulling the needles out as the stitch is worked, but the method is hardly the same, and belongs to a chapter on knitting.

3. Repairing gentlemen's undergarments, such as pants and vests.

4. Joining a new sleeve into a jersey suit.

5. Securing the top and bottom of a patch, which might be placed in any of the above garments.

6. Any instance in which it is necessary to join one set of loops to another.

III. Preparation of Material.—Hold the work on the right side, and at right angles to the way it is knitted or woven, so that the columns of web run right and left. With the eye of a needle unpick half a loop at a time, across the width of the web, and as the thread becomes about an inch long, cut it off, as it is apt to drag the loops out of place. The left thumb should be pressed just at the back of the loops as the thread is withdrawn. The loops should be perfectly clear and distinct, so that they could be picked up with a knitting needle. If the sides of the web are intact, such as they would be in a patch, or in the repairing of a ladder, the upper row of loops will have *one whole* loop less than lower row, but to compensate for this there will be a half loop at each end of the upper row.

A wool needle is recommended for use, being less likely to split the loops.

IV. Position of Work.—Grafting is worked upon the right side of the garment, and from right to left.

Hold the pieces one above the other, over the first finger of left hand, so that the loops face the worker, and that the *loops* in the lower row are exactly opposite the *spaces between* the loops in the upper.

V. Directions for Working.—Commencement. As web is such elastic material, it is advisable to leave a finger length of thread, and secure this when the work is done, by darning the end neatly on the wrong side ; any attempt at making a strong beginning often results in dragging the loops out of place.

The Stitch.—Bring the needle out from the back through the middle of the first loop in the lower row ; take two loops in the upper row horizontally, back to back (the first loop taken should be the one just on the right-hand side of the lower loop, and if the sides are intact it will only be a half loop), the two

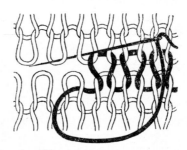

FIG. 183.—GRAFTING IN PROGRESS.

inside parts of the loop will be *on* the needle, and the two *out-side* parts *under* it. Draw through gently so as not to dis-arrange the loops—now take two loops in the lower piece in just the same manner—the first loop taken in this row should be the one in which the work was started—the needle is thus inserted in each loop *twice*.

Continue working alternately upper and lower row, the last loop of the preceding stitch in each row being the first one of the next.

The diagram (Fig. 183) illustrates the stitch in detail.

Fastening Off.—Darn the end up and down on the wrong side, also the thread left at the commencement.

To Graft a Purl Loop in the Lower Row to another Purl Loop in Upper Row.—This requires great care. It is sometimes necessary to work this in a calf of a stocking when connecting a seam stitch.

If the purl loop in the *upper* row be examined, it will be seen that it consists of *two half* loops, which the grafting thread must connect and form into one.

It is worked as follow : Completely finish the plain loop before the seam stitch—insert the needle into the purl loop *from the front* pointing it to the N.E. as it were, and at the same time take up *from the back* the right-hand *half* of the purl stitch in the upper row and draw through carefully—turn the needle round so that it points to the S.E., and insert it downwards into the *left*-hand half of the purl stitch in the upper row, at the same time bringing the needle *from the back* through the purl stitch in the lower row. (These half purl stitches are very much inclined to fall back quite behind the other loops, therefore it is as well to look at the wrong side at this stage and see that the newly-grafted purl loop corresponds with the other loops, which it will do if the directions have been followed.) Put the needle into the first plain stitch after the seam loop in the lower row, from the back, and then to the right-hand side of the plain loop in the upper row, and go on as usual.

Points for Criticism are—

1. Mending thread unsuitable to the web.

2. Thread drawn too tightly, or left so loose that the loops do not match surrounding web.

3. Incorrect formation of loop.

4. Untidy fastenings.

CHAPTER XLII

TAKING UP A LADDER IN STOCKING-WEB, OR MENDING A BREAK FORMED BY A DROPPED STITCH

I. Description.—What is known as a " Jacob's ladder " is caused by—

1. The breaking of one or more loops, which drop bar after bar rapidly until they form an endless number of strands one above each other, with a loop or more at the bottom, or " on the first rung," so to speak.

2. Dropping a stitch in knitting, and letting the loop run down.

3. Faulty weaving by the machine, *i.e.*, slipped loops. This is generally rectified, in a way, before the web leaves the factory.

II. Method of Picking Up—

1. A crochet hook ;
2. A pair of knitting needles ; or
3. The head of a pin or darning needle.

Any of the above can be used for this purpose.

Hold the right side towards the worker. Put the left hand into the stocking, keeping the ladder over the forefinger.

1. To Use a Crochet Hook.—Insert the hook in the loop, draw the bar just above it through the loop, and so on till each bar has been treated in turn. The head of a pin may be used in the same way. This plan is similar to working " chain " in crochet.

2. To Use Knitting Needles.—Insert one needle into the loop, as for ordinary knitting, with the right-hand side of the loop *over* the needle. With the other needle lift up the bar just above the loop on to the needle, and draw the loop *over* the bar from *left* to *right*, which will form a new loop ; and continue this plan of working till all the ladders are used up. This is to form a " plain " loop. A " purl " loop is slightly different. It may be either picked up on the *wrong* side, like a plain loop, or if held right side to the worker, the bar must be on the needle first, and then the loop. Draw the loop over the bar from *right* to *left*.

3. The Darning Needle may be used if the above-named implements are not at hand. Put the eye of the needle from the worker, upwards through the loop, then pass the needle

202

between the first and second bars, and bring it out in the loop again, with the first bar on the needle as a fresh loop. Draw out the needle and insert it again as before. This plan is more likely to split the bars unless very carefully done, but it is a ready method. Whichever way has been chosen for picking up the ladder, when all the bars are drawn through, the loop should be grafted in its place, and a few rows of plain darning, or Swiss darning, preferably the latter, worked around the grafting for strengthening.

To fasten off, run the thread up and down the loops for a few rows on the wrong side. If several loops are dropped, it is well to place a pin in those not under treatment, to prevent them running further. Begin with the right-hand loop, and when that is drawn up to place, fasten it by a pin or thread while the other loops are picked up.

Fine Webbing.

On a very fine stocking it will be almost impossible to pick up the ladders as described for coarse web ; in this case, the ladder must be darned by passing the needle *through the loop,* and taking a bar and missing a bar alternately all down the ladder, being careful to darn a sufficient distance beyond the hole for strength. In the second row, take up the bars missed in the first row, just as in the common method of darning, and strengthen the break.

III. Points for Criticism are—

1. Loops badly picked up.
2. Strands split.
3. Grafting clumsy, and general appearance untidy.

CHAPTER XLIII

STOCKING-WEB DARNING

I. Introduction.—Before this kind of darning is attempted it is necessary that Swiss darning and grafting should have been mastered—there is, then, little to learn, but a deal to practise.

II. Description of the Darn.—It should resemble the surrounding fabric in appearance, and if the thread used to mend the hole is similar to the original material, the darn will be hardly noticeable, as it is really hand-weaving a patch. It is necessary that the top, bottom, and sides of the hole be strengthened by Swiss darning, which is done as the work proceeds. As all " web material " consists of woven loops, the stitch for mending must imitate it exactly.

III. Method of Working the Stitch.—This is best taught by means of strands formed upon a card, and the loops worked around these strands (*not* through the card). Plain and purl can be taught in this way, also intakes for the calf of a stocking. The latter should not be attempted until proficiency is attained with the plain and purl stitch.

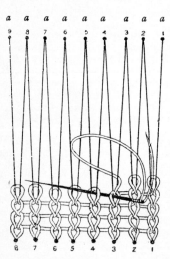

IV. Description of Card.—Fig. 184 shows the usual method of preparing the card. It must be noticed that the dots in the lower row are not *opposite* those of the upper row. These dots represent the *loops* of the web, and it will be remembered from the chapter on " Mending a Hole (common method) " that the loop faces the space between the loops, and *vice versâ*; therefore the dots are in the same relative position, so that the foundation strands stretch from upper to lower dots in the form of a V.

V. Directions for Stranding.—Use crochet cotton, or thread a little finer and of the same colour as that with which the darn is to be worked. If the strands are allowed to remain in the work when the darn is finished (this is optional), it is necessary that the same colour should be used. On medium

FIG. 184.—STOCKING WEB, PLAIN STITCH, AS WORKED UPON A CARD.

The bar of thread which is shown between each stitch would not be noticeable if the loops were closer together, as they would be in the web. They are spread out in the diagram to show the working.

204

cotton webbing embroidery thread is by far the best for the purpose, No. 35 is suitable for stranding, and No. 18 for working the stitch. Make a firm knot. Begin at the *bottom right-hand* corner.

Bring the needle out at No. 1.   Put it in at No. 1a

,,	,,	,,	,,	,,	2a	,,	,,	,, 1
,,	,,	,,	,,	,,	2	,,	,,	,, 2a
,,	,,	,,	,,	,,	3a	,,	,,	,, 2
,,	,,	,,	,,	,,	3	,,	,,	,, 3a
,,	,,	,,	,,	,,	4a	,,	,,	,, 3

and so on, finishing at the *bottom left-hand* corner.

If this stranding has been accurately done, all the strands will be on the *upper* side of the card, and *two* threads in *each* dot, except at the *sides of the top*, which in webbing will correspond to *half loops*.

VI. The Plain Stitch.—The first row of loops on a *card* must be made rather *loosely*. Bring the needle out at dot 1,* pass it under the two foundation strands (*not* through the card) from right to left, and put the needle in again at the same place as in starting—draw down, leaving a loop about ⅙ in.—this forms the first stitch. Bring the needle out at 2, and repeat from * to the end of the row, when each dot should have a loop above it.

2nd Row.—Turn the card completely round, so that what formed the top before is at the bottom now, the strands being *below* the working instead of above it as in the first row, and the thread on the *under* side of the card. Pass the needle *through* the card (but it must not pierce the card again throughout the work, unless for a join in the thread) and bring it out in the *middle* of the right-hand loop, and *between* the strands. Put the needle under the two foundation threads, and in again *exactly in the middle of the first loop and between the strands*, bringing it out in the middle of the second loop, passing under the third and fourth strands. Put the needle into the middle of the second loop and out in the third loop, and so on to the end of the row.

To Turn the Corner.—Put the needle in the last stitch as if about to make another, but instead, pass the needle perpendicularly through the middle of the last loop, taking up the *top* of the loop on the needle and keeping the needle above the working thread. Fig. 187 shows the end of the thread in the last stitch.

3rd Row.—Turn the card so that it is in the same position as for the first row. Work several rows until the stitch can be done regularly, so that it has the appearance of plain knitting.

VII. Preparation of the Material for Mending.—It is advisable to use webbing of medium coarseness for practice.

Hold the work the right side uppermost, and handle it very gently.

1. Cut a perpendicular slit (only about ½ an in. for practice purposes).

2. At the *bottom* of the slit unpick the web first *to the left* and then *to the right* exactly as described for " Grafting," p. 199, Heading III, and *three* loops are sufficient *each* way. The last loops in each side must be perfectly clear, neither joined on to the mass of web nor with an end in them (the ravelling threads must *not* be cut off, but put to the *wrong* side, and cut off or darned down when the work is completed).

3. Unpick the upper part of the slit similarly, but the corners will have a *half-loop* right and left on each side of the top, so that if there be *six whole* loops at the bottom there should be *five whole* loops and two halves at the top. (Fig. 185 shows nine loops at the bottom, but this makes too large a hole to work as a time test.)

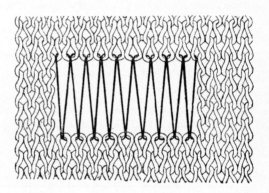

FIG. 185.—HOLE PREPARED AND STRANDED.

All the loops must be *perfectly clear*, so that they can be picked up with a knitting needle.

The worn sides, which should appear like shutters to a window, must **neither be unravelled nor cut off,** but turned under on to the wrong side so as to present a *perfectly straight edge ;* and if by chance the edge should not form a *straight column of loops*, another stitch must be unpicked to allow of this. It will, therefore, be seen how advisable it is to make a *small* hole to start with, as it rapidly increases in size.

This preparation should be well practised on a small piece of web, till it can be quickly arranged.

A better grasp can be obtained over the work if the material needing repair be tacked *right* side uppermost upon a piece of card or paper. Fig. 185 shows the hole prepared and stranded. Particularly notice the half loops at the top, which correspond to 1a and 9a in Fig. 184. The pieces of web which are turned under would not be seen on the right side.

VIII. Stranding the Hole.—This is worked exactly as on the card, only *into the loops*. Make a knot and pass the needle through the card, and up through the first loop at the *bottom right-hand corner* (the loops should be taken on the needle *as in grafting, i.e.*, back to back). Insert the needle at the top half-loop (No. 1*a* on the card), and bring it out in the next loop, then back to the first loop at the bottom, and so on alternately top and bottom, finishing at the *bottom left-hand corner*. There should only be *one* strand in each *half loop*. There is a tendency to contract the hole in stranding, and so strain the loops. Be very careful to avoid this, or the appearance of the darn will be spoiled.

IX. Commencement of the Work.—It is necessary to strengthen the top, bottom, and sides of the hole by rows of Swiss darning,

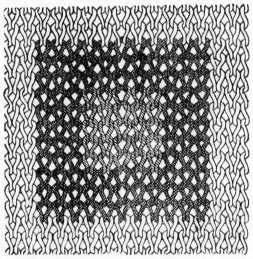

FIG. 186.—SHOWING A HOLE FILLED IN. THE DARK SHADING REPRESENTS THE SWISS DARNING.

which is done as the darn progresses. The whole loops form the *bottom* of the darn. Bring the needle out a few rows *below* the hole, and a few loops to the *right* (say, three or four). Swiss darn across for the same distance on the left-hand side, and continue till the hole is reached.

X. Filling the Hole.—Work the stitch exactly as described under Heading VI. The loops will require a little arranging with the needle as the work proceeds. Be careful to make the filling-in stitch match the original loop in point of size. Swiss darn the sides as each row is worked, *i.e.*, after the stitch is worked across the strands, with the same cotton darn over a few loops at the sides—turn the work round and darn the next row, and so on across the hole. When the hole is filled up, *the last row must be grafted* to the loops which carry the foundation strands. Swiss darn above the holes to correspond with that below.

The turned-back sides need not be caught in with the Swiss darning, but it is not of much consequence.

XI. Finishing Off.—Cut the knot of the foundation strand. Remove the work from the card. Darn the ends of the mending thread neatly on the wrong side. The sides which were turned back may be now cut off close, as the Swiss darning at the sides is sufficient strengthening. It is optional whether the foundation strands be removed, but if taken out they should be *cut* and gently drawn, not pulled. Their removal adds to the elasticity of the darn, and makes the mending like the original web, so perhaps is preferable ; but objections are often raised,

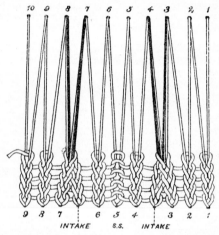

FIG. 187.—SHOWING SEAM STITCH AND INTAKES.

because should the strands have been caught in forming the loops, the stitches will give way. Fig. 186 shows a darn complete.

A darn of an irregular shape, as in Fig. 184, should be worked as soon as the square or oblong can be done accurately.

Some people prefer that the sides should be unravelled, each end threaded separately, and darned back in a slanting direction on to the wrong side of the fabric. In this case, it is not necessary to Swiss darn at the sides, but to work exactly as on the card, till there are as many rows of loops, minus one, as there are stitches at the sides, the last row is then joined by grafting. Thread each end and catch up the side loop of the mending, and darn down on the wrong side. If the end is short it is better to run the needle in, and thread it afterwards. This is an exceedingly neat and flat method, but is more tedious to work on account of the threading process.

A good darn can also be made by darning back each end, and Swiss darning only one stitch on each side of the hole.

XII. The Purl Stitch.—In order to put in a patch in the calf of a stocking, it is necessary to know how to work a purl stitch, and to form intakes. The purl stitch is best taught upon a card. Prepare as for the plain stitch. All that it is necessary to bear in mind is, that purling is worked exactly the *reverse way* to plain, *i.e.*, where the cotton passes *under* the strands in the plain stitch it is taken *over* in purl. Complete the plain stitch which adjoins the purl (suppose the card to be held with the strands, *above* the work), put the needle into the middle of the loop *from the front*, pointing it to the N.E.—pass the cotton over the strands, and bring it through the middle of the loop *from the back*, pointing it to the S.E., then proceed with the plain stitch. When the strands are below the working, the direction of the needle will be reversed, viz., S.E. and N.E. Fig. 187 illustrates the purl stitch.

XIII. Intakes.—Here the method of stranding is slightly different, as allowance must be made for the additional loops previous to the decrease. The intakes should also be taught upon a card. Suppose, for example, one set of intakes has to be worked. The lower row will have *two* more loops than usual. One plain stitch is kept each side of the seam loop, and in stranding the loop next this plain stitch must be passed over. The two odd loops can be stranded separately after the other foundation is formed. (Fig. 187.)

When filling in the hole on stocking-web material, the seam stitch presents a difficulty. The method of grafting a purl stitch is described in the chapter on " Grafting " (p. 200). The seam loop must be *stranded* in *exactly* the same manner. It is not unusual to see an otherwise good darn spoilt by an incorrect grafting of the seam stitch.

To work the intake row. Finish the fourth loop before the seam stitch, this will leave three clear loops ; take up the second upon the needle, then bring the needle up through the third loop (by this means the third loop will be *above* the second). Pass the needle round the four strands, and put it into the *middle* of the loops, still keeping the third on top of the second. This forms the intake *before* the seam stitch. To work the decrease *after* the seam stitch, proceed as follows. Complete the one plain on the left-hand side of the seam. Pass the needle through the second loop, and then through the third in the ordinary way. Make the third loop rest on the top of the second, put the needle under the four strands and insert it into the middle of the loops ; be sure that the needle does actually pass *into the middle* of these two loops, otherwise when the stranding is withdrawn the loops will drop. The point of the needle will be an assistance in the arranging.

If two sets of intakes be needed, of course two loops on either side of the seam stitch must be left when putting in the foundation strands.

The strands which bear the intakes can be cut out as soon as a few rows beyond the decreasings are worked, otherwise they are in the way for the ordinary working.

XIV. Uses of Stocking-web Darning.—For repairing any kind of coarse stocking-web fabric, such as jerseys, pants, knees of knitted stockings, or any part of an article which would look unsightly if the hole were darned by the common method.

N.B.—It is not intended to be used on fine web, as at the best of times it is a process requiring a large amount of care, practice, and skill, and an unlimited quantity of patience and perseverance, and time may be much more profitably employed on more useful needlework.

CHAPTER XLIV

PATCHING KNITTED OR WOVEN WEB

I. Remarks.—Before attempting the above work, it is necessary to practise grafting and Swiss darning. This kind of patching is an excellent method of repairing coarse web. It does not take a long time to work, and has the advantage of making a worn garment wearable, but not unsightly with a quantity of darning. It is necessary to have a piece of material of the same texture and colour as the original, for unless the loops are of the same size the patch will not be flat.

II. Preparation of the Hole.—There are two or three methods of treating the sides of the hole.

First Method.—Begin on the right side. Do not cut away the worn part, but unravel till a row of loops can be obtained at the top and bottom of hole sufficiently strong to bear the new thread.

The loops must be clear and distinct, so that they could be picked up with a knitting needle if desired.

Be sure the sides are quite straight, *i.e.*, the column of loops on the right side, one above each other, with the *half* loop at the right and left-hand corners of top row. Turn back the sides of the hole and tack or pin them down.

III. Preparation of the Piece for Insertion.—This should be a few loops larger than the size of hole as it so quickly unravels. Have a clear row of loops top and bottom, and the sides cut evenly.

IV. To Graft the Patch.—It is advisable to tack the work on a card or stiff paper, right side uppermost. Commence with the bottom row of loops and graft these to the garment. It is better to leave all ends on the wrong side and neaten when the work is finished.

Unravel the upper part of the patch to fit the hole, remembering that grafting will *add* a row of loops.

Graft the upper part of patch to the garment. The sides should now be treated.

Turn under the sides of patch so that the web of the garment and patch seem continuous (a few stitches in ordinary sewing cotton will keep this in place).

About 6 or 8 stitches of Swiss darning are necessary ; 3 or 4 on the patch and the same on the garment. Fine thread is recommended for this, else bulkiness is inevitable.

Remove the work from the card. Turn to the wrong side and darn in all ends as for a plain darn.

The Swiss darning has rendered the sides sufficiently strong, so that the piece of web turned back can be cut off.

Second Method.—This is not quite so tedious as the last, but the sides are more unsightly.

The top and bottom of the patch are grafted in the same way as before. The sides of the hole and the patch should be cut quite evenly, and closely button-holed with sewing cotton the same colour as the web, about two loops deep. It is well to run a few strands down the sides to prevent fraying. The knots of the button-hole stitches are then sewn together on the wrong side.

Third Method.—Treat the top and bottom of the patch and the hole as before, then unravel the sides quite straight, and leave the ends hanging of both patch and garment. Turn to the wrong side, lightly overcast the edges to keep them firm. Thread the needle with the end from the garment, and darn it on to the patch in a slanting direction, then the end from the patch, and darn on to the garment, and so on alternately. If the end be short, it is best to darn the needle in, and thread it afterwards.

This method makes a very flat patch, and is really " grafting " in every sense of the word, but has the effect of trying one's patience to the utmost.

The first method is the best for coarse material, the second for fine.

The beauty of the patch lies in its perfect flatness when complete.

NOTE.—The above methods are only suitable for skilful workers, but the housewife who has to repair woven garments quickly should patch *coarse* webbing in the same way as if it were flannel, viz., herring-boning. *Thin* webbing might be repaired by sewing and felling.

The ridges of the loops in garment and patch should agree as regards their weaving.

A patch may be placed on the wrong side and darned down to the garment, and the right side of the garment darned also.

CHAPTER XLV

FINE DRAWING FOR REPAIRING CLOTH

I. Description.—This is a method of darning applied to cloth or thick materials not liable to fray.

Strictly it is a tailor's art, but as its application is often necessary upon boys' clothing, and for other domestic purposes, a description of the method of working will perhaps be of service, considering that if successfully done the mend will be almost invisible.

II. Preparation for Mending.—Sharp scissors are necessary. Cut the edges of the hole perfectly clean and even, either square or oblong, and a patch the *exact* shape of the hole. The patch should match the material surrounding the hole, both as regards selvedge and way of the nap.

Hold the garment wrong side uppermost, and lightly fix the patch in place with a few large stitches of cotton. Be very careful to keep all perfectly flat. Use fine silk, which should exactly match the shade of the material, or the ravellings of the stuff are also suitable. A long, fine needle is recommended. Place one side of the patch along the forefinger of the left hand, so that the two edges are kept close together, while the thumb rests upon them.

III. Method of Mending.—Begin at the left-hand side. Slip the needle between the thickness of the cloth, and bring out about ⅛ in. from the edge of garment. Pass the needle, pointed *from* the worker, slightly in a slanting direction, to ⅛ in. from the edge of the patch, only taking up *half* the thickness of the cloth, so that no stitch will be seen on the right side, and only just the place of the insertion of the needle on the wrong. Point the needle *towards* the worker and bring out again on the garment. Draw the thread sufficiently tight, so that the edges neither overlap nor gape, but *just meet*. Continue working in this way, taking a stitch alternately on either side till the patch is inserted. Special care is necessary at the corners, to prevent any dragging or puckering.

IV. Finishing Off.—When the mending is complete, remove any fixing threads, place a damp cloth upon the wrong side, and press with a warm iron.

V. Remarks.—This is a very effectual method of repairing a tear in cloth, or inserting a patch, especially if there is not likely to be much strain upon the part. It is rather a tedious process, and requires some amount of skill in execution, but amply repays if well done.

A tear in cloth may often be mended in this way if the edges are not frayed much.

CHAPTER XLVI

THE REPAIRING OF HOUSE AND TABLE LINEN

I. The Care.—The expression " household linen " is a comprehensive one, and admits of wide extension. It is not limited now, as was formerly the case, to table linen, sheets, and pillowcases ; but is generally understood to include all articles in use for domestic purposes, whether made of linen or cotton.

A good housekeeper will always take a great interest in the repair and replenishing of the linen press. In olden times the family linen had often as much store set by it as the family plate, and even in our day it is not unusual to hear the remark, " That belonged to my grandmother."

The worth of a housekeeper may often be estimated by the condition of the linen, not so much by the number of articles, as by the state of repair in which each is kept.

To mend successfully requires judgment and skill, which can only be acquired by practice.

Many people, who excel in the " making " of garments, have not the same reputation for " mending," because this branch of household management requires the display of that rarely exercised quality — common sense — a faculty which is not always inborn. All articles for domestic use should be carefully stored in a linen cupboard, the shelves of which should be lined with clean paper. The cupboard must not be placed against an outer wall, in case of the penetration of damp ; the most desirable position is near a wall which is in connection with the kitchen flue, as the warmth retained by the bricks is the best preventive from mildew.

A list of the articles should be hung up inside the cupboard, which will show the contents at a glance.

Certain times of the year should be chosen for the entire overhauling of the linen press, so that the supply may be kept up annually with comparatively a small expense.

The weekly or fortnightly round of repairing must go on uninterruptedly year in year out, as by this means a housekeeper may save many shillings by extending the time an article will wear. When linen is returned from the wash it should be overlooked for places needing repair, and hours of mending may be ultimately saved if rents and cuts are lightly drawn together before washing, in order to prevent them " going further," which invariably happens after washing and wringing. Table linen should always be mended previous to washing.

In a well-arranged linen cupboard, each set of articles should have a selected place. When linen is returned from the wash, after having been aired and mended if necessary, each article should be placed at the bottom of the pile. This arrangement will secure uniformity in the wear.

Old house linen should always be preserved, the finer kinds for bandages and wounds, and the coarser for kitchen and house rubbers. Old muslins are suitable for poultices and for straining purposes. Worn calico articles are useful as wrappers and dust covers. Old blankets and quilts, too thin for bedroom service, may be turned to a variety of uses in the house.

II. The Repair.—SHEETS generally begin to wear in the middle, and directly a weakness is noticeable they should be turned sides to middle. This is effected by cutting the sheet down the centre, sewing the selvedges together to form a new middle, and hemming the outer raw edges. By this means the time of wear may be considerably lengthened. Ends also are sometimes turned to middle. Thin places can be darned neatly with flax thread, or patching may be adopted at any stage of wear.

Bolster cases are often made from worn sheeting, also coverings for pillow slips, used merely for keeping the tick clean.

TABLECLOTHS.—Flourishing thread should always be used for mending purposes. (*See* p. 186.)

Three kinds of repairing may be noticed—

1st. **A clean cut** made by the careless use of a knife. The method of mending is described under the head of a " Cross-cut."

2nd. **A thin place** caused by wear. This should be darned, as described in the chapter bearing upon this kind of work (p. 168).

3rd. **A Tear or Hole.**—A very successful plan of mending a worn tablecloth, and a more careful and neat way than treating as for a calico patch, is as follows—

Procure a good piece of cloth, matching the original as nearly as possible in texture and pattern.

1. Cut this $\frac{3}{4}$ in. larger than the size the patch is required.

2. Place this right side downwards upon the wrong side of the worn cloth, paying attention to the way of material, and the matching of pattern as near as is possible.

3. Fix carefully close to the raw edge, taking care that the patch is perfectly flat.

4. Commence at the left-hand corner and darn down the edge of the patch on to the edge of the cloth, exactly as for strengthening a thin place. A good $\frac{1}{4}$ in. of darning on both patch and cloth is generally sufficient. Leave very short loops, about $\frac{1}{10}$ in., to allow for shrinkage in washing.

5. Darn all round the four sides of the patch similarly.

6. With a penknife or blade of the scissors gently raise up any loose edges of the patch, cut these close, and smooth the darning with the round blade of the scissors, or the bowl of a spoon.

7. Turn to the right side and cut away the damaged material, leaving ¼ in. margin from the lower edge of the darning on the wrong side.

8. Darn down the raw edges and trim as on the other side.

This is rather a slow process, but well repays for the trouble, and is an excellent method of repairing worn table linen.

When damask is beyond use as tablecloths, the best portions may be turned to account for tray cloths, finger napkins, small cloths to put under pie dishes, fish napkins, and numerous other purposes which will suggest themselves to a housekeeper, as old table linen is useful to the last rag.

Towels may be treated similarly to table linen.

Quilts and **Toilet Covers** are generally darned with white darning cotton.

Muslin Curtains.—These should be mended when " rough dry," but holes are best treated if lightly drawn together previous to washing.

A person who can mend thoroughly well is sure to be a good housekeeper in other respects. Nothing shows painstaking industry more than good darning, as, though necessary work, it is sometimes, perhaps, rather monotonous ; but a " Stitch in time, saves nine " is a homely proverb, and one's conscience has often to repay for care and trouble bestowed ; besides, there is always a sense of satisfaction in having done a " duty."

CHAPTER XLVII

OPENINGS IN GARMENTS

I. Introduction.—There are many ways of arranging openings in garments by the addition of false hems or false pieces.

The principal point to be kept in mind when cutting the placket or opening, is to so arrange the sides that the opening may come *in the middle* of the garment (if it is intended to be there) when completed.

Different garments require different methods of preparation, according to the position of the placket or opening.

II. Length of Openings.—These may vary with different parts of the garments, but the following can be taken as the approximate length.

Front of a Shirt.—The length of the collar when fastened.

Wrist Opening in a Shirt.—$\frac{1}{2}$ length of the wristband, or rather less than $\frac{1}{3}$ length of the seam of the sleeve.

Side Opening in a Shirt.—Length of the armhole measured from the front width.

Back of a Baby's Nightgown.—About 5 in. below the waist

Side of Children's Drawers.—$\frac{1}{3}$ length of the garment before any shaping is done.

Placket of Petticoat, Skirt, or Frock.—About $\frac{1}{3}$ or $\frac{1}{4}$ of length

MADE IN GREAT BRITAIN AT THE PITMAN PRESS, BATH
C7—(H.814)

BOOKS ON DRESSMAKING AND KNITTING
ETC.

THE COMPLETE KNITTING ROOK
With Patterns and Easy-to-Follow Diagrams for Knitting Every Garment for Woman, Child, and Man.

By MARJORY TILLOTSON. Edited by DAVIDE C. MINTER.

Shows how to work all kinds of stitches, from the ordinary plain and purl, to those used for more elaborate openwork designs. It gives minute instruction in the details of tension, measurement, proportion, etc. Many helpful examples showing the application of stitches and the methods of drafting out patterns are given, with suggestions for suitable colour schemes.

210 pp.   **5s. net**   **Illustrated**

HOME DRESSMAKING
Every Woman's Practical Guide to the Art of Making Smart Clothes. With Chapters on Sewing for Babies and Children, and Renovations.

By AGNES M. MIALL.

This is the most helpful guide for all who make their own clothes. It gives useful information on fitting, cutting out, making up, etc., is profusely illustrated and deals with constructive principles that can never get out of date. There are also chapters on making lingerie, tailored blouses, etc., and how to carry out successful renovations.

190 pp.   **5s. net**   **Illustrated**

THE ART AND PRACTICE OF MENDING
By J. M. HOLT.

A practical and detailed guide to the art of mending, darning, and renovating of personal wear, household and decorative fabrics, with numerous diagrams illustrating the methods described. Every method of mending is included, from darning stockings to patching large holes and tears. The book contains much useful reference material for all teachers of needlework and for training college students.

88 pp.   **3s. 6d. net**   **Cloth**

SIR ISAAC PITMAN & SONS, LTD., PARKER STREET, KINGSWAY, W.C.2

A SELECTION OF
BOOKS ON EMBROIDERY

A Manual of Handmade Bobbin Lace Work

By MARGARET MAIDMENT, Cert. R.S.A.N., City and Guilds of London, etc.

Describes the methods and processes involved in making Torchon, Cluny, Honiton, Beds-Maltese, and other Bobbin Laces, from drafting and pricking patterns to fittings and embroidery finishings.

In crown 4to, cloth gilt, 188 pp., with 172 examples and working diagrams. **15s.** net.

Colour Pattern for Embroidery

By ANNE BRANDON-JONES.

A practical and comprehensive handbook planned to help needle-women untrained as designers to prepare simple stitch and pattern decoration suitable for household fabrics and articles of dress.

In crown 4to, cloth, 72 pp., with 12 colour plates and 12 diagram sheets. **12s. 6d.** net.

Portfolio of Embroidery Pattern Designs

By JOAN H. DREW.

A handy collection of examples in design based on a large number of classical models.

Size 12 in. by 9 in. **2s. 6d.** net.

Embroidery and Design in the New Stitchery

By ELIZABETH GLASIER FOSTER.

Consists chiefly in the building up of beautiful but simple patterns by designing from single *motifs*.

In foolscap 4to, cloth, illustrated. **2s. 6d.** net.

Embroidery and Pattern Design

By HANNAH FOWLER and G. F. CRAGGS.

The book contains a wealth of suggestions for articles to be embroidered and for various designs.

In foolscap 4to, cloth, 166 pp., illustrated in colour and black and white. **7s. 6d.** net.

Constructive and Decorative Stitchery

By ELIZABETH GLASIER FOSTER.

The principle of sewing described in this book combines two processes in one, i.e. construction and decoration.

Size 5¾ in. by 7½ in., cloth, 146 pp. **4s. 6d.** net. Fourth Edition.

SIR ISAAC PITMAN & SONS, LTD., PARKER STREET, KINGSWAY, W.C.2